VIRTUAL SELLING

PREVIOUS BOOKS BY THE AUTHORS

INSIGHT SELLING (Wiley, 2014)

What do winners of major sales do differently than sellers who almost win, but who ultimately come in second place?

Mike Schultz and John Doerr, bestselling authors and world-renowned sales experts, share the answer in *Insight Selling: Surprising Research on What Sales Winners Do Differently*. Their findings are based on the study of more than 700 business-to-business purchases made by buyers who represented a total of $3.1 billion in purchasing power.

In *Insight Selling,* Schultz and Doerr outline exactly what you need to do to transform yourself and your team into insight sellers.

RAINMAKING CONVERSATIONS – *Wall Street Journal* Bestseller (Wiley, 2011)

Conversations make or break everything in sales. Every conversation presents an opportunity to find new opportunities, win new customers, and increase sales.

In the *Wall Street Journal* bestseller, *Rainmaking Conversations: Influence, Persuade, and Sell in Any Situation,* Mike Schultz and John Doerr provide a proven system for leading masterful sales conversations that fill the pipeline, secure new deals, and maximize the potential of your accounts.

Based on research, decades of experience, and in-depth interviews with leaders of the most successful sales organizations, *Rainmaking Conversations* presents a guide to help sellers build rapport and trust from the first contact, uncover the full set of buyer needs, make a strong impact case, craft the best solutions, and close the deal.

VIRTUAL SELLING

HOW TO BUILD RELATIONSHIPS,
DIFFERENTIATE,
AND WIN SALES REMOTELY

MIKE SCHULTZ, DAVE SHABY, ANDY SPRINGER

FOREWORD BY JOHN DOERR

Thirty-Five Group Press

Virtual Selling:

How to Build Relationships, Differentiate, and Win Sales Remotely

© 2020, Mike Schultz, Dave Shaby, Andy Springer. All rights reserved.

Published by 35 Group Press, Boston, MA

978-1-7348839-0-9 (paperback)
978-1-7348839-1-6 (ebook)
978-1-7348839-2-3 (audiobook)
Library of Congress Control Number: 2020907969

www.raingroup.com

Publishing consultant: David Wogahn, AuthorImprints.com

TABLE OF CONTENTS

FOREWORD

During my lifetime I have worked as an accountant (for only six months), copy writer, direct mailer extraordinaire (at least in volume), salesperson, senior sales executive, CEO, expatriate managing director, and entrepreneur. While all were important steps on my journey to eventually co-founding RAIN Group almost twenty years ago, perhaps the most enlightening chapter in my career history was that of publisher for a small business book press.

During that time, I had the opportunity to read hundreds of manuscripts from aspiring as well as established authors who were certain they had written the ultimate view of whatever sea change was at that time creating turbulence in the business world.

A few of those manuscripts were good, and I considered them briefly before finally passing on them. Many were superficial, and those ended in the bin. A very exceptional few brought clarity, insight, and value to the reader. I enthusiastically read those to the end and published them. In the process, I learned a great deal that helped me navigate those 10 present challenges and many future ones.

Today we are faced with another sea change of historical enormity: a pandemic crisis that has impacted every aspect of every life throughout the world. Of course, this, too, has resulted in a new surge of advice and guidance in the form of hastily thrown together articles, white papers and business books about how we should work in a virtual, remote, and geographically distanced economy. Most of these books, if I were still evaluating manuscripts, would join their brethren, from years ago, in the bin.

But not *Virtual Selling: How to Build Relationships, Differentiate, and Win Sales Remotely*. It was with great excitement and anticipation that I approached my first read of this dynamic book. I knew that Mike Schultz, my co-author of three earlier books, Dave Shaby, who I have had the privilege and pleasure to work with and whose career I followed closely for years, and Andy Springer, a brilliant student and practitioner of selling and the teaching of selling who I turn to whenever I need a creative and insightful view of the world of sales, did not throw this book haphazardly together overnight. I knew that their combined years of experience and their fresh insight into virtual selling would make this book a standout in a growing library of guides to virtual selling. What was going to happen anyway, had happened. But Mike, Dave, and Andy have already proven their track record and knowledge in virtual sales. That experience and acumen is what makes up *Virtual Selling: How to Build Relationships, Differentiate, and Win Sales Remotely*. For that reason, this is the book that sellers need the most right now as the pandemic raises many questions about the future of the art of selling.

Schultz, Shaby, and Springer use the RAIN Group Sales Competency Wheel as a foundation to describe how the transition to virtual selling affects all aspects of sales from how best to sell value through the entire sales cycle, how to build relationships, how to understand the process of selling virtually, and how to provide leadership to a developing sales culture.

Throughout the book, the authors artfully show what steps of traditional selling will remain the same, and how the implementation of those steps will be radically different from live, in-person selling. Most importantly, the trio provide step-by-step guidelines showing you exactly how to adapt to the new conditions brought on by the growing changes in work habits in the last decade, as well as the overnight switch to virtual sales that were swept in on the pandemic. Their book discusses how to implement, how to adjust, and how to make virtual selling work for every seller who is open to this change.

Schultz, Shaby, and Springer provide detailed approaches to the new selling skills required when selling remotely. And it is not just about selling on the phone, which many have been doing for years, but rather using technology the right way so informed sellers can stand out from those who will stumble their way along thinking that virtual sales will just be a passing adaptation to a passing global crisis.

I invite experienced sellers who want to "sharpen the saw" and those just getting into selling to enthusiastically read, cover to cover, *Virtual Selling: How to Build Relationships, Differentiate, and Win Sales Remotely*. It is one of those exceptional few books that I once would have published with great enthusiasm, to benefit today's virtual sellers.

John Doerr, Co-Founder, RAIN Group
Co-author, *Insight Selling: Surprising Research on What Sales Winners Do Differently, Rainmaking Conversations: Influence, Persuade, and Sell in Any Situation,*
and *Professional Services Marketing*
Wellesley Hills, Massachusetts
May 2020

WELCOME TO THE NEW WORLD OF VIRTUAL SELLING

The Pot Boils

In 2005, we interviewed and studied a few hundred sellers and buyers of business-to-business products and services. When we asked about prospecting through LinkedIn, and the importance of sellers maintaining a great LinkedIn profile, we got a very firm and consistent answer.

"Executive-level decision-makers," the sellers told us, "don't use social media. So, it's not important."

Stop chasing the shiny new technology penny, they told us, and focus on what really makes a difference in actual business-to-business selling.

Sounds funny today. Indeed, in a recent study of close to 500 buyers conducted by the RAIN Group Center for Sales Research, we learned that 82 percent of them look up sellers on LinkedIn before replying to sellers' prospecting efforts.

It took about ten years for this "executives don't use social media" belief to disappear. Like the proverbial frog in a pot of cold water that heated lazily to a boil*, people didn't really notice the change happen—but now, it's undeniable.

Likewise, the shift to virtual selling was slowly warming to a new future that would likely have taken a business generation to materialize fully. We'd been working on this book's content for about two years before the novel coronavirus hit the scene. Once it

---

* A myth, but one that persists and is useful for our tale.

nit, we witnessed the pot go from a simmer to a full-on boil over about two weeks.

Our friend the frog could have jumped out of the pot if the temperature changed quickly and, presumably, headed back to the home pond and enjoyed life as previously known. No can do for sellers—jump out as they may want to do, there's no familiar home to jump to; the old pond is gone.

Many sellers find themselves flailing around in the boiling virtual waters of change. Some will boil out of the selling profession quickly, others a little more slowly. But if they don't do what they must, they're headed out the door one way or the other.

There's only one choice for sellers who plan to achieve sales success: Adjust to the change.

Master the art of virtual selling.

The Enemy in Our Midst

Before the novel coronavirus, virtual selling was less newsworthy, but still critically important to those who had to either a) do it or b) suffer through sellers attempting it and failing miserably.

How bad is the situation? Buyers tell us that sellers are only falling short in two parts of virtual selling: the virtual part and the selling part. ~~Talk about unmitigated disaster.~~ Sellers definitely have a long way to go.

With the "selling" part, buyers tell us that the sellers who interact with them virtually are not likely to interest them in the sellers' offerings at all. Sellers don't lead thorough needs' discoveries. Sellers are deficient in crafting and communicating compelling solutions, creating compelling value cases, inspiring buyers to take action, and to choose the seller over their competition.

The "virtual" part is just as bad. (Remember, this is not according to us, but according to buyers. Hard data on this coming soon.) One buyer told us that when it comes to the *experience* of working with sellers it seems like they are "showing up every day in schlubby suits with their shirts untucked and their shoes not shined. It's like they aren't even paying attention." The complaint cover the gamut: how sellers build relationships, how they lead video conference meetings, their facility with web technologies and support materials, and their overall approach in trying to influence the buying process.

Shaking their heads at the deficiencies of virtual sellers, buyers confess that if they could get the products and services they needed, and if they get the advice and decision support to help them succeed, they would buy.

The interesting point is that we heard about the sellers' lack of skill and competence with virtual selling *before* the coronavirus pandemic quarantines that started in March 2020. This was a problem even among sellers who weren't driven by necessity, they *opted* to use web and video conference technologies for selling.

As we write this, more than 90 percent of business-to-business sellers,[1] and a great majority of business-to-consumer sellers, have been forced, due to the circumstances of the quarantine and spread of the virus, to interact virtually.

And it's ugly. At least that's what buyers are saying. In April 2020, the RAIN Group Center for Sales Research surveyed 528 buyers, sellers, and sales leaders regarding the state of virtual selling. What we found was even more troubling than we expected.

Not only do buyers say sellers are not very effective when it comes to virtual buyer interactions, but they're doing a remarkably poor job in the areas that most influence buyers' purchase decisions, such as leading a thorough needs discovery, listening, showing what's possible, and making the return on investment (ROI) case clear—among others.

Some sellers believe virtual selling is temporary. One seller we spoke to recently said, "When it goes back to normal, I won't need to do this anymore." Maybe. But when we say "maybe" we mean maybe in the same way we tell a seven year old that maybe he'll be a professional baseball player. It's not likely. The switch to virtual selling may not be absolute, but it's likely to become a permanent part of most sellers' routines.

As for going back to "normal" economically, the recession following the financial crisis of 2008 was corrected comparatively quickly to other historic recessions, but it still took seven or eight years for many buyers to back off of their protective, tight-with-a-buck, defensive-buying postures. They pushed prices. They had a high bar for value. Buyers made it difficult for sellers because *they needed and expected more from sellers*. This never went away.

Going into 2020, the economic environment was generally strong, but you still couldn't sell like people sold in 2002 and expect to succeed. Starting in 2008, things changed and selling became more challenging. Some sellers never caught up. While investment and spending loosened up, the bar that buyers set for sellers had risen permanently.

The bar just shot up again: In addition to the need for sellers to drive meaningful buyer value, they must master virtual selling.

We at RAIN Group are in the interesting position of participating in decision-making discussions with leaders at both mid-size companies as well as some of the largest, most well-known companies in the world. In the spring of 2020, many companies laid off sales people. Did they lay off the ones who had value figured out? Who had virtual selling figured out? Who knew how to work from home (or any place) and be extremely productive regardless of the conditions around them? Not so much.

As for the rest? Virtual pink slips.

If you don't want this to be you or the sellers on your team, if you want to succeed in the new world of virtual selling, the first step in fixing the problem is clear: Know your enemy.

Selling can't go on like it used to. The enemy is the status quo.

The Widening Success and Failure Gap

Increasing numbers of sellers will fail given both the challenging economic environment and the durable shift to virtual selling. But for those who adapt to the new world, great success awaits.

Why? Because buyers will find a smaller subset of sellers who are engaging, impressive, and worthy of building relationships with.

Consider the following. Among the most challenging areas of virtual selling, out of eighteen possible challenges, are:[2]

- Gaining buyer's attention and keeping them engaged virtually (91 percent somewhat to very challenging)
- Changing buyer's point of view on what's possible or how to solve a problem (89 percent somewhat to very challenging)
- Developing relationships with buyers virtually (88 percent somewhat to very challenging)

The sellers who figure out virtual selling will impress buyers. They'll get first crack at the buyers' opportunities. Buyers will reach out to sellers they respect for ideas on how to approach their challenges. Buyers will give these sellers access. Thus, when the sellers reach out, they'll be able to proactively drive opportunity, help buyers to shift and set new priorities, and attack challenges with better approaches.

With the bar raised, fewer sellers will succeed. Those who do will stand out from the crowd more than ever and enjoy unprecedented success.

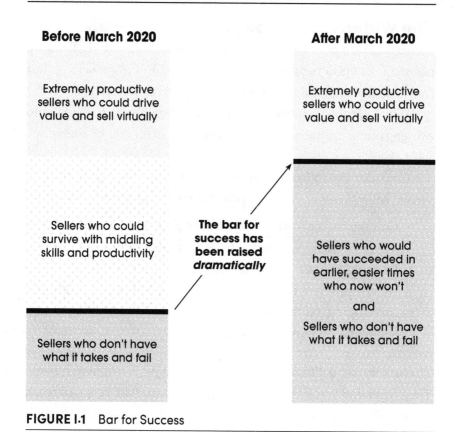

FIGURE I.1 Bar for Success

But to stand out, sellers need the skills to find opportunities and close deals—and these skills are lacking.

In our *Top-Performing Sales Organization Benchmark* study, we analyzed selling skills of teams across twenty-six industries globally to assess what the Top Performers do differently than The Rest to achieve the best results, including: higher win rates (62 percent vs. 40 percent), meeting annual sales goals, setting more challenging sales goals, and achieving maximum prices in line with the value they provide.

We analyzed data from 472 sellers and executives representing companies with sales forces between ten and 5,000+ sellers. Top Performers represent the top 20 percent of our database; The Rest are the bottom 80 percent.

We found that less than half of sellers had core consultative sell-ing skills (e.g., understanding needs, crafting compelling solutions based on need), only about one-third of sellers had good time man-agement and productivity skills and habits, and only about one-third of sellers could be considered advanced consultative sellers who drove ideas and helped buyers change their thinking on how to approach solving their challenges.

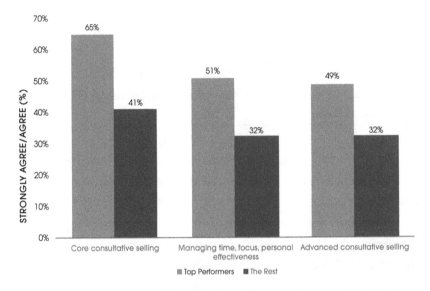

FIGURE I.2 Sellers Have the Skills They Need to Find and Win Business Consistently and at a High Level

Meanwhile, for virtual selling, the skills situation is even worse. In our *Top Virtual Selling Challenges and Priorities* research, here's how business-to-business buyers ranked ten seller behaviors with the greatest impact on their purchase decisions versus the effective-ness of sellers in those areas.

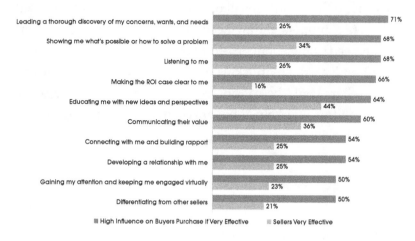

FIGURE I.3 Sellers' Virtual Effectiveness and Influence on Purchase According to Buyers

For the most part, buyers said only between one-in-three to one-in-four sellers are very effective in the virtual medium for these essential sales skills.

In a tough business environment with completely new selling dynamics, the gap between success and failure is wide, but the opportunity for sellers to succeed is real.

The Opportunity

Imagine for a moment, as economic conditions rebound, buyers go from a defensive disposition—spending little and hoarding cash—to offensive. Their businesses start to smooth out, they've right-sized, they're feeling more stable. They start looking for opportunities to make a difference, either driving more cost savings and efficiencies, striving for new growth opportunities, or seeking innovation.

Buyers will begin to take calls from sellers. They'll inquire about products and services. They'll try to figure out what they can do on their own with their in-house teams. They'll evaluate their positions and know where to spend, and how to approach driving value that will make a difference.

The sellers who can deeply understand buyers and their goals, provide ideas and new thinking, make the ROI case and build confidence that initiatives will succeed will find themselves winning consistently. But it's likely that buyers won't be taking as many in-person meetings as they used to. They'll be evaluating online, talking to sellers over video conference calls, expecting virtual collaboration, and anticipating virtual presentations.

Consider as well that sellers who, until this point, had a lot of planes, trains, and automobiles to get to in-person sales meetings are now spending less time in airports, on jammed freeways, and circling parking garages. Sales leaders report their sellers who transition to the virtual realm are leading two-to-three times more meetings as they used to.

Buyers expect and require virtual selling. And sellers, at least those who get the hang of it, will lean more heavily on virtual than ever before—by choice.

The trouble is, too few sellers are getting the hang of it. The faster that changes, the more quickly their fortunes will turn around.

Taking Advantage of the Changes

Q. How many psychologists does it take to change a lightbulb?
A. Only one, but the lightbulb has to want to change.

How do sellers gain new skills and master the new dynamic of selling virtually? It starts with the first step: being the lightbulb that wants to change. Ask yourself the following questions to see if you're willing to change.

With the extra time gained from less travel and a smoother schedule between meetings, could I:

- Spend more time researching buyers' needs, goals, and challenges?
- Customize my agendas, meetings, materials, and strategize for each buyer specifically?
- Make stronger ROI cases for buyers to act—and act now?

- Implement big-play strategies for large opportunities that deserve the extra pursuit intensity, going above and beyond to inspire buyers?
- Spend more time collaborating with buyers, both driving value and strengthening my relationships with them?
- Craft more specific, customized solutions for each buyer and their individual needs?
- Spend more time prospecting to fill the pipeline with my existing accounts and for new greenfield opportunities?

And, in general, could I:

- Capture and maintain buyer engagement in virtual meetings exceptionally well?
- Come across as exceptionally professional and impressive in virtual meetings?
- Strengthen my rapport-building through online technologies and meetings that eliminate antiseptic impressions and, instead, convey the warmth of an in-person meeting?
- Become proficient in the technologies of online communication and collaboration?
- Bring together buyers in different locations by running more effective large-group client meetings?
- Become more knowledgeable about buyers' inclinations and preferences through online technologies like online document sharing and behavior tracking that provide a sense of what resonates best with them?

If you want your answers to be yes to all of the above, it will likely take some work to get there.

But there's never been a better time to master virtual selling. We three authors of *Virtual Selling* are about the same age. When we started working twenty years ago, the idea of working from home for anyone—buyers and sellers alike—was stigmatized. Working from home two decades ago signaled a lack of professionalism. "Real" businesspeople worked at "real" offices.

Those days are gone. You can sell remotely now, to and from a home location, and it's perceived as normal. It's the business model of the current era. New and better technologies have emerged in the last several years, and the changing views on work-from-home give virtual selling many advantages over face-to-face selling.

While gradual changes have made virtual selling acceptable, recent events have also made virtual selling a necessity. The challenge comes when sellers lack the skills to achieve successful results. Since you're reading this book, we assume you're here to conquer that challenge and take advantage of the changes.

Now, like no other time, you should be selling virtually because it works.

How This Book Is Organized

Our primary goal in writing *Virtual Selling* is to give you a practical guide, rich with tactical advice for how to succeed in selling when you aren't there face-to-face.

In each section of this book, you'll find brief overviews of core selling topics, regardless of whether they're executed face-to-face or virtually. Discussion about how to "virtualize" sales skills without briefly overviewing the skills themselves would leave out critical concepts required to understand the subject.

The lion's share of content, however, focuses on how to apply each concept in a virtual selling context.

Throughout this book, you will see a rating called the Virtual Selling Divergence Scale. This scale measures the relative difference between face-to-face selling (which we also refer to as in-person selling) and virtual selling, and is applied to various selling situations (e.g., Needs Discovery). The scale flags areas of virtual selling that require the highest level of change. Pay particular attention to *why* we assign the specific rating.

For those of you who are experienced sellers, some of our overall sales advice may sound familiar. Some of the concepts, though, have evolved over the years (e.g., Case-Making, Advanced Consultative/Insight Selling) so take care to glean conceptual nuggets you might find helpful.

For those of you who are newer to selling, the concepts themselves may take some time to digest. For most sellers, straightforward as the concepts may be, they take years to master. If you find there's a concept you want to learn more about, we've made references to other materials and provided online lessons and concepts in the *Virtual Selling* book tools on the RAIN Group website (http://raingrp.com/VS-BookTools). These will be noted throughout.

SECTION I:

SEISMIC SHIFTS IN THE WORLD OF SELLING

Three seismic shifts recently changed the role of the seller.

1. Buyers have no need for sellers who don't drive value: The emphasis on seller value has been a gradual shift since the internet tipped the scales of information, leverage, and power from sellers to buyers.
2. The novel coronavirus pandemic of 2020 drove a radical, immediate shift to virtual selling: Even seasoned sellers were unable to adjust to the nearly overnight change from face-to-face selling to virtual selling in the face of quarantine.
3. After a decade of growth, the world found itself in an economic downturn that, depending on the sector, is likely to have long-lasting implications.

These shifts, some more gradual, and others within the span of a mere two weeks, made selling significantly more difficult. As the coronavirus shutdowns took place, an already challenging role became even trickier.

However, much as some sellers might want to revert to the way it was, that won't happen. The ever-increasing demand for sellers to add value, and the move to virtual buyer-seller interaction, will endure.

According to research conducted by RAIN Group's Center for Sales Research during the pandemic,[1] sales organizations were conducting a greater proportion of their sales activities virtually.

Pre-pandemic, only 27 percent of respondents reported conducting more than half of their sales activities virtually. During the pandemic, 71 percent were conducting more than half of their sales virtually. That's a 163 percent increase. This was a major shift in a very short period of time.

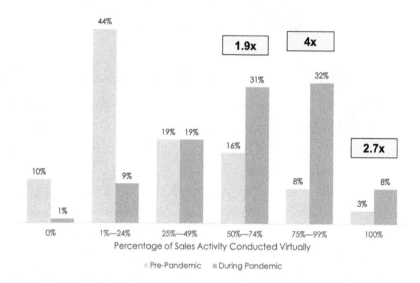

FIGURE I.4 Virtual Selling Pre- and During Pandemic

According to multiple studies by firms like Bain and McKinsey, virtual selling will continue to be the new normal even when face-to-face selling is an option. Virtual selling is here, and here to stay.

CHAPTER 1

GREAT SELLING, DONE VIRTUALLY

Great Selling

People overcomplicate selling. Selling, like anything, is best when it's simplified, but not so simplified that you miss something critical.

At RAIN Group, we see that great sellers are great at some mix of the competencies (skills and attributes) represented on our Sales Competency Wheel℠.

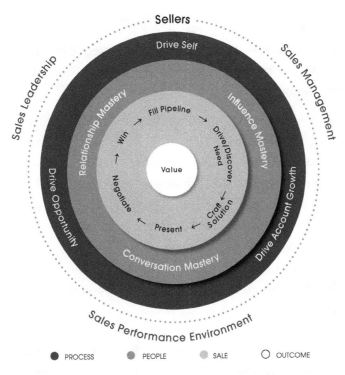

FIGURE 1.1 The Sales Competency Wheel℠

For both in-person and virtual selling, the same sales dynamics are at play. Sellers just need the skills to approach and accomplish them differently. Let's first cover what the competencies of great sellers look like.

Value

At the center of the Sales Competency Wheel[SM] is value. According to our research, *The Value-Driving Difference*,[1] sellers who drive value have a higher win rate (54 percent vs. 45 percent) and are more likely to grow revenue (90 percent vs. 72 percent). The organizations that drive value tend to retain top sales talent at higher rates (73 percent vs. 61 percent).

Everything sellers do should drive value for a buyer. Sellers, however, can't drive much value unless a buyer engages. This is where the sales cycle comes into play.

Sales Cycle

The job of a successful seller is to guide buyers through the sales cycle, providing value at every step. Everything connects to value. That means you must:

- Fill the pipeline by inspiring buyers with the value you can bring to the table.
- Discover needs and uncover what's going on to bring your buyer the most value. Drive needs with insight selling to give buyers an idea of possibilities they didn't know existed.
- Craft a solution to give buyers the best value.
- Present value as persuasively as possible.
- Negotiate based on value over price.
- Win deals when buyers see the value is worth the effort and cost.

As you can see, the entire sales cycle is designed to drive value. But selling doesn't take place in a vacuum, and isn't a purely academic exercise. If you want to put opportunities into the sales cycle—do well with them—you need to succeed with people.

The next layer of the wheel deals with people.

People

Many sales pundits have said that technology will soon replace sales people.

We don't think so. We do think buyers and sellers will interact through technology much more than ever before, but it's not technology that drives sales—it's the people.

To the extent that sellers can succeed with people, they will succeed as sellers. To make this happen, sellers must be great at:

- Developing and deepening relationships with buyers,
- Influencing buyers and driving decisions down specified paths, and
- Leading conversations to run an efficient sales cycle, be influential, and develop relationships.

Process

For anything in the Sales Competency Wheel℠ to happen consistently—and happen consistently well—sellers must succeed with three processes:

1. Driving account growth: Sellers need to uncover where the biggest opportunities are, how they're going to put them in the pipeline, and how they'll win them (hint: it all comes back to value). Account growth begins with the value you can bring to your account over and above what you're currently doing with them.
2. Driving opportunities: If you have a big opportunity, you need a process to win the opportunity on the big stage.
3. Driving self: You need to focus on being the most productive and performance-oriented person you can be.

17

Making this all happen with energy, enthusiasm, and passion over time comes down to culture, which is the next layer of the wheel applicable to sales leadership.

Culture

Your sales culture is the tide that raises (or lowers) all boats. Three key factors that drive culture are sales:

1. Sales leadership,
2. Sales management, and
3. Sales performance environment.

These influencers of culture bring our Sales Competency Wheel℠ full circle. When sales leadership, sales managers, and your sales environment work together to prioritize value for buyers, results improve. (See the *Virtual Selling* book tools section of the RAIN Group website to learn more about each component of the Sales Competency Wheel℠.)

If you can build a sales organization that attends to each element of the Sales Competency Wheel℠—value, sales cycle, people, process, and culture—you'll have a sales organization to be envied.

The bad news, according to buyers, is that virtual sellers are falling short across the board.

Making the ROI case clear to me	16%	84%
Differentiating from other sellers	21%	79%
Gaining my attention and keeping me engaged virtually	23%	77%
Developing a relationship with me	25%	75%
Connecting with me and building rapport	25%	75%
Listening to me	26%	74%
Leading a thorough discovery of my concerns, wants, and needs	26%	74%
Negotiating with me	27%	73%
Using tools (e.g., demos, whiteboarding, spreadsheets, video) that demonstrate the value of their offering	30%	70%
Showing me what's possible or how to solve a problem	34%	66%
Collaborating and interacting with me virtually	34%	66%
Communicating their value	36%	64%
Using technology when leading a virtual sales meeting (e.g., presentations, audio, visuals, demos, web meeting software)	40%	60%
Educating me with new ideas and perspectives	44%	56%
Reaching out to me to set meetings by phone, email, etc.	59%	41%

■ Agree　■ Disagree/Neither Agree Nor Disagree

FIGURE 1.2　Sellers' Virtual Effectiveness According to Buyers

Indeed, across the virtual sales cycle, sellers have a long way to go. But this is good news for you. Why? Because the gap between the skilled and the unskilled is, at this moment, wide. Thus, those who take the lead and close the gap will achieve outsized success.

Take the Lead

Selling virtually versus selling in-person requires sellers to be more strategic, more deliberate, more focused, and more proactive than ever before. These attributes are critical to success. The mantra we use that captures the essence of what sellers need to do to succeed in virtual selling is "Take the Lead."

No sitting back. No allowing your pipeline, your opportunities, and your relationships to unfold organically. Doing these things in face-to-face selling are not necessarily advisable, but they're a death knell in virtual selling.

Five key areas in selling (four for sellers, one for sales managers and leaders) are significantly different in virtual selling. Sellers must take the lead in:

1. **Self:** While virtual selling often means selling without meeting in-person, it also means working from home or, if at the office, working there exclusively without venturing out much. It's easier to lose focus and fall into unproductive ruts when you're not driving or flying from meeting to meeting, and when you're staring at a screen all day. To succeed in this area, sellers must focus on their:

   - Motivation: Manufacture motivation even when you don't feel like you have it, and maximize it to its fullest extent both short and long term.
   - Focus: Take control of your time and become impossible to distract.
   - Execution: Get the most done in the time available.

   Motivating yourself and staying focused was especially challenging during the pandemic, with 79 percent of sellers and sales leaders saying they were experiencing extremely or somewhat negative sales effects because of the pandemic and resulting economic environment, and only 11 percent saying it was somewhat or extremely positive.

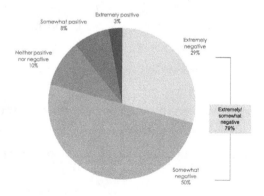

FIGURE 1.3 Impact of Pandemic on Sales

2. **Meetings:** Meetings themselves literally happen through a different medium virtually versus in-person selling. To succeed with meetings sellers must take the lead in:
   - Purpose: Making sure each meeting achieved planned outcomes.
   - Preparation: Making sure each meeting is orchestrated for success.
   - Professionalism: Making sure buyers develop the impression that sellers have both competence and gravitas, and are modern in their approaches.

3. **Relationships:** In face-to-face selling, there are networking events, office meetings, coffee and meals, and working on-site at client locations. Relationships often develop organically, without much proactive effort. In a two-dimensional world, however, it's completely up to the seller to make the space for, and create the conditions conducive to, building and deepening the right relationships.

4. **Case-Making:** Selling is inherently about change. If you want to be successful in selling, you need to make the case for change to your buyers. There are five cases sellers must make to drive change.

   1. Priorities: Sellers need to make sure that buyers choose the right top-of-agenda priorities. Make sure buyers know they should: *"Do this, not that."*

   2. Approaches: Once buyers choose the right priorities, they need to tackle them the right way. Make sure buyers know they should: *"... this way, not that."*

   3. Impact: Sellers need to make the case for impact, as impact drives buyer urgency and action. Impact is emotional *and* rational, typically focused on the ROI case. Make sure buyers believe in the most powerful reasons, or, *"because."*

4. Decisions: Buyers must act, and do so with urgency. They need to know what to do next and when. In other words, *"Act now, not later."*

5. Partners: Finally, once buyers plan to act (do this), in a certain way (this way), to achieve excellent results (because) with urgency (act now), they need to choose their partner. Thus, finishing the flow *"… with us, not them."*
   "Do this, not that … this way, not that … because. Act now, not later … with us, not them."

5. **Sales Team Leadership:** For sales leaders, virtual selling requires material changes in how they lead their teams.* They need:
   o Rhythm: Establish the right frequency, length, agendas, and types of interactions with sellers.
   o Roles: Play the five roles of a sales coach (motivate, focus, execute, advise, and develop).
   o Conversations: Interact with their teams through virtual media as powerfully as they do when face-to-face.

If sellers take the lead in the first four areas, and managers do so in the fifth, the odds of success climb sharply. Neglecting to do so will likely lead to failure. We don't mean to overstate the point, but virtual selling is patently another dimension compared to face-to-face selling. As the eminent W. Edwards Deming said, "Change is not necessary, but neither is survival."

Another Dimension

Virtual selling is a completely different sensory experience than face-to-face selling.

---

* In *Virtual Selling* we focus on selling, not sales leadership and coaching. For a white paper specifically covering the topic of managing and coaching virtual sellers, visit http://raingrp.com/VS-BookTools.

- Sight: You can see the person, but you can't read them like you could if you were in a real room together. In the virtual world, you can only see one-fifth of them. (Maybe they're wearing pants. You'll never know.) But, you'll only see them if they turn their video on. If they can figure out how to turn their video on. And, you'll only see them if their lighting is okay, which it often isn't. They can also see you, and while they look right at you, they may be replying to emails, reading websites, and muting themselves while they chat with their colleagues.
- Sound: You can hear them—if you both have a decent connection and nobody has inadvertently muted themselves. And they can hear you (if you have a decent mic), as well as your kids, your neighbor's lawnmower, and Freido your little chihuahua.
- Taste, Smell, and Touch: Selling isn't all about office meetings, it's also about everyday meetings at restaurants and industry events with the breakfasts, lunches, coffees, dinners, sports and recreation outings, and so on that go with them.

  If you're not at events and conferences, sure, you miss the bialys and the fancy lattes, but you also miss the chance opportunities that happen, and you miss the ability to make the sort of connections that have you saying when you return to the office, "The travel and fees were totally worthwhile because I met … "
- Mind: Virtual selling is not only a dimension of sight and sound, but of mind. Affecting, changing, and deeply influencing buyer's minds is vital to selling success. Decisions buyers make to do one thing versus another or nothing at all. Decisions to tackle challenges one way versus another. To select one provider over another. Then there are the smaller ways the mind is involved in selling. Sellers gaining buyer

attention and keeping it during meetings. Judgments that buyers make about you one way or another.

In virtual selling, the differences here are so significant it would be too much to list them all out (at the moment—we do later), but consider gaining and holding buyer attention at meetings: If you were in a conference room with them would they look you in the eye, yet actually be responding to emails with their laptops open? This won't happen much in a face-to-face meeting in a conference room. Yet on web meetings, it happens all the time when sellers don't hold the buyers' attention. Indeed, the *engagement threshold* is that much higher for virtual meetings.

In-person selling is three-dimensional (3D); selling virtually is two-dimensional (2D). Selling in 2D requires the seller to orchestrate *a sensory experience that is rich, attention-grabbing, rationally engaging, and takes buyers on an emotional journey that ends with a decision in the seller's favor.*

Specific Areas Where Virtual and In-Person Selling Differ

Topic	In-Person or Blended	Virtual
Prospecting	Office environments built for peer and manager support and accountability. Tech environment good for prospecting (e.g., office phone).	Isolation leads to lack of focus and accountability. Peer and manager support less present. Technology environment may have holes.

Topic	In-Person or Blended	Virtual
Rapport and Relationship Building	Can happen organically. Chats before meeting starts; chats after. Chats over coffee. Chats at a meal. Chats at a conference. Physical presence is naturally more connection-building in 3D vs. 2D.	Conversations are naturally more tactical and mechanical. Live meetings that start at 10 a.m. in an office may actually begin at 9:45 with 15 minutes of catch-up conversations. 10 a.m. virtual meetings tend to start at 10 or so, jump right in, and end without rapport-building chat.
Needs Discovery	Easier to have organic back and forth.	Needs to be more organized. Gaps in conversation tolerated less. Interactivity with visuals even easier than face-to-face.
Demonstrations, Idea Communication, Storytelling	So much easier to show physical product, draw on white board, or share.	Not as easy to write, show, share in an organic way. Easy now to share a screen, but collaboration through white boarding, giving demos, or making the experience grabbing from a sensory perspective is that much harder virtually.

Topic	In-Person or Blended	Virtual
General Sales Meeting Management	Everything happens more organically. To the extent many sellers are organized at all they can come across as impressive.	As a great percent of communication is nonverbal, sellers who do not use the medium well allow the flat screen to translate into a flat feeling. Orchestrating meeting kickoff, making space for rapport, managing video and other tech, manage timing and time left, orchestrate files and visuals, all more challenging virtually.
Proposal and Finalist Presentations	Easier to be interactive. Can read the room.	More challenging to take the lead to be interactive, connecting, read the room. Default is talk and present slides; many sellers don't change the dynamic away from seller-presenting-one-way-dog-and-pony show.

Topic	In-Person or Blended	Virtual
Account Development	Straightforward to set meetings to either create or share ideas. Relationships in place, so often happens organically on-site. Easy to create reason to be on-site. Easy to collaborate in meeting rooms.	Not on-site, no organic discussions that often lead to aha moments and buyer action items. Not on-site, more difficult to collaborate without white boards and meeting rooms.
Email and Messaging	Supplemental to live discussions. Many sellers focus on live communication, and keep email to a minimum; short. Sellers not focused on writing as a selling medium.	Writing for communication and for *conversation* is a core, integrated part of virtual selling. Challenging to read buyer through their written interactions to see what they prefer for how to interact. (Some buyers are really impressed by good emailing and documents. Others not so much.) Many sellers not prepared *must be prepared to be compelling and conversational via email.*

Topic	In-Person or Blended	Virtual
Work Environment	Your office or theirs. Typically maintained well. Everyone dressed for work. Collaboration easy.	Technology critical for visual, audio, collaboration. Kids, families, barking dogs. Space at a premium, originally designed for work. Blended boundaries of work and home.
Productivity	Offices and spaces set up for work, focus. Peer support for focus. Break areas and work area delineations.	Distraction central. Fuzzy boundaries between work/ nonwork spaces. Isolation and self-distraction common.

At this point, you may feel like the deck is stacked against you in virtual selling.

In fact, it's not.

Imagine several key areas in selling:

- **Networking and Prospecting:** *You used* to spend thirty hours in travel, $1,700 in expenses, and two nights away from your family to generate four high-quality industry connections and five leads for new business.

  Now, virtually, you do the same, at no expense, in sixteen hours from your desk.

- **Relationship—From Surface Level to Personal Connection:** *You used to* talk to a few people a week at offices around meetings and over coffee and meals. Coffee and meals, while "quick" would inevitably kill a half a day adding in the commutes and location switches.

Now, virtually, you have one in-depth conversation per day with people you are just getting to know, for forty-five minutes each.

Consider the math if you had the same number of meetings: five meetings a week at three hours each for in-person selling, that's 900 minutes or about two full days. Five *virtual* meetings a week at forty-five minutes per meeting is 225 minutes, or about half a day. Nine hundred minutes minus 225 is 675. That's eleven hours saved while you have two more relationship-focused meetings.

- **Relationships—Collaborating to Drive New Ideas:** *You used to* drive or fly to a client site, spend time organizing and setting up for, say, a two-hour meeting and then collaborate in a conference room. Without that travel and setup, virtual sellers save a *ton of time.* But most sellers don't focus on time and productivity gains. Instead, they focus on a belief that collaborating online just isn't the same. It isn't as good. It isn't as rich.

  Now, virtually, you collaborate via online collaboration tools and it works just as well or better. Don't believe us? It's true and has been documented. According to the *Harvard Business Review,* online collaboration can be *even more effective than in person.* More on this in Chapter 10, How to Collaborate with Buyers Virtually.

- **Needs Discovery:** *You used to* prepare before a meeting to plan your questions or write them on a notepad, but it was difficult to look at them during a live meeting, and you couldn't look at any reference sheets to aid in your questioning or answers about offerings.

  Now, virtually, you have prepared questions in front of you, as well as your questioning and information reference sheets. The buyer can't see them so it's not bad form to have them in front of you.

- **Making the Impact Case:** *You used to* gather some data in a meeting, and then present back an ROI case at some other time via presentation or proposal (that is, you would if you wanted to make the most sales). However, it wasn't interactive because the buyer wasn't part of building it.

  Now, virtually, you have real-time, collaborative impact modeling sessions where you calculate the return on investment. Since it's collaborative, the buyer is more tuned in, more impressed, and more likely to act because they crafted the case with you, versus passively receiving it later.

- **Delivering a Proposal Presentation:** *You used to* impress your buyers in person with extremely well-crafted presentations that weren't just presentations, they were an experience that set you apart from all others.

  Now, virtually, you do the same. However, many sellers don't know the various strategies that are uniquely suited to virtual presentation and experience creation and, so, miss out on maximizing this opportunity.

- **Populating Your CRM:** *You used to* take notes at meetings, type them up, and put them in your customer relationship management (CRM) system at a cost of hours per week

  Now, virtually, you take and record notes in your CRM nearly in real time. Why not, you're on a computer already. More time saved, better notes, happier sales managers.

- **Meetings per Month:** *You used to* have a total of one-and-a-half sales meetings of various sorts per day. With the driving, flying, and extra work for CRM, keeping up with the stringent scheduling and activity was exhausting, something you'd have to fight in order to perform.

  Now, virtually, you average three meetings per day, literally *doubling your meeting output* with *zero degradation in meeting quality*. (Note, the actual numbers don't matter here. What matters is most virtual sellers report being able to double or triple their meeting numbers with virtual selling versus face-to-face.)

FOR LEADERS: A COST IMPACT MODEL
FOR VIRTUAL SELLING SAVINGS

Chapter 6 of this book is titled Making the Impact and ROI Case. In our experience, making the ROI case in a way that a chief financial officer would find compelling is exceptionally difficult for many sellers. (And, indeed, buyers report that only 16 percent of sellers do this very effectively.) Here's what an ROI case might look like for transitioning to virtual selling.

Impact Model: Face-to-Face vs. Virtual

Note: Numbers rounded for illustration purposes

Current State: Face-to-Face			Future State: Virtual		
Pipeline Metrics		Conversion Rate	**Pipeline Metrics**		Conversion Rate
Meetings	230		Meetings	345	
Pipeline	115	50%	Pipeline	173	50%
Proposals	46	40%	Proposals	70	40%
Wins	20	42%	Wins	30	42%
Avg size	$100,000		Avg size	$100,000	
Total sales per seller	$2,000,000		Total sales per seller	$3,000,000	
# of sellers	100		# of sellers	100	
Sales per year	$200,000,000		Sales per year	$300,000,000	
			Increase	**$100,000,000**	
Avg sales mtgs per day	1		Avg sales mtgs per day	1.5	
Selling days per year	230		Selling days per year	230	
Meetings per year	230		Meetings per year	345	
% days travel	50%		% days travel	10%	
Travel days per year	115		Travel days per year	23	
Travel costs per day	$1,200		Travel costs per day	$1,200	
Travel costs per seller per year	$138,000		Travel costs per seller per year	$27,600	
Travel costs per yr total	$13,800,000		Travel costs per yr total	$2,760,000	
			Cost Savings	**$11,040,000**	
			Total Impact	**$111,040,000**	

56% revenue growth by transitioning to virtual selling

Two things to note:

- All we did was cut travel costs and increase the number of meetings a seller has from one to one-and-a-half per day, something easily achievable if a seller cuts travel time for sales meetings, say, from 50 percent to 10 percent of their time.
- We kept all other assumptions the same, which is also easily achievable and beatable for those who build the right virtual selling skills.

Visit the *Virtual Selling* book tools section of the RAIN Group website to download an interactive version of this Virtual Selling ROI calculator (http://raingrp.com/VS-BookTools).

Chapter 1 Key Takeaways

- **In our new reality,** sellers who take the lead and excel virtually stand to win big as the skills gap widens between high performers and the rest.

- **Driving value for buyers remains** the central focus for successful sellers. In a virtual setting, throughout the sales process, **value-driving** skills will stand out.

- **Five key areas** where sellers or sales managers need to take the lead:
  1. Self: Developing discipline in a changing sales environment
  2. Meetings: Managing the dynamics of virtual settings and new technologies
  3. Relationships: Building rapport and trust in 2D vs. face-to-face
  4. Case-making: Guiding and convincing buyers virtually to change perspectives, and to choose your new approach, right now
  5. Sales team leadership: Managing a sales culture to succeed in a virtual world

CHAPTER 2

CONSULTATIVE SELLING *OVERALL* HAS CHANGED— HOW SELLERS MUST ADAPT

Influence from Afar

No two ways about it—in-person meetings differ intrinsically from virtual meetings. A live meeting carries with it a certain gravitas, regardless of the agenda and who's in attendance, and people feel more connected as a result of their physical presence in the same room.

Virtual meetings, on the other hand, feel less important, the connection between people often as tenuous as their internet connection.

In the Sales Competency Wheel℠ outlined in the previous chapter, the words "Influence Mastery" appear in the people section. We contend, and will talk about it quite a bit throughout *Virtual Selling*, that selling is about change management. The seller leads the change and must be a master of influence to be successful.

The more gravitas someone has and the greater their connection to other people, the easier it is to influence and drive change. That's two strikes against selling in the virtual environment: It inherently has less gravitas, and it's more challenging than live meetings to make personal connections.

While these might be two strikes against the virtual environment, they're *not* two strikes against you, and they need not hinder your success. In fact, the opposite is true; virtual selling will help you succeed. Here's why: Most other sellers will be slow to recognize the changed dynamics. They won't take the lead, and they won't sell (and influence and drive change) effectively in a virtual environment. If you adapt before others do, you can widen the gap between you and the rest.

Throughout this book, we cover how you need to adapt your selling approach to the virtual environment. In this chapter, more than the others, we focus on how most sellers need to adapt their selling approach generally, conceptually. If, as you read, you feel like skipping the conceptual shift and getting to the tactical advice, move ahead to the following chapters. But for now, big picture, here's how consultative selling is no longer what it used to be.

Not Your Father's Consultative Selling

Since Mack Hanan coined the term in 1970, consultative selling has been the most widely accepted and pursued sales approach. For the ensuing forty years, advice on selling has mostly been a variation on the consultative selling theme.

In the past handful of years, however, selling in general (not just virtually, but overall) has changed more than it had in the previous forty years put together. It has changed so much that variations on the consultative selling theme have been replaced by numerous calls to blow it all up and do something completely different. In the foreword to our RAIN Group book, *Insight Selling*,[1] Neil Rackham a pioneer in consultative selling had this to say about the explosion of turn-selling-on-its-head approaches:

> I ask you to forgive me a moment's bitching if I pick out a particularly unhelpful trend in many of these about-to-be-come-best-selling business books, especially those in sales, that use what I call the *Armageddon selling* formula. The approach goes something like this: "Everything you've ever learned about sales is wrong and, unless you stop doing it instantly, your sales efforts will shortly die in agony. There is, however, one simple cure that I have discovered. It is…"

and here the author puts in a pitch for the appropriate magic bullet...

He goes on to say:

> The Armageddon approach to sales doesn't help anyone. When, for example, a serious journal like the *Harvard Business Review* publishes an article titled "The End of Solution Sales," it damages the credibility of all involved. The sales field has been growing up nicely in recent years: It can live without this kind of overstatement.

Who's right? Should we blow up consultative selling and replace it with something completely different? Or, does it just need a few changes to make it still relevant today?

We know buying has changed overall and will continue to do so. Selling must change with it. The question is: How? Let's take a close look at the evolution of consultative selling and what sellers need to do to win in the new sales environment, virtual or otherwise. We also note how these changes apply to virtual selling, but reserve most virtual selling advice for the rest of the book.

What Is Consultative Selling?

There are many definitions of consultative selling. This one from Study.com is representative of the most common themes across definitions:

> Consultative [selling] is a selling method in which the salesperson spends time with the customer to understand the problem the customer is trying to solve and then recommends a solution that will specifically address that problem. It's different from a traditional sale in that it involves suggesting a solution to a problem, rather than a focus on selling a specific product.[2]

In a recent article, twenty-six experts weighed in on how to develop a consultative sales approach. Most focused on ways to make the definition above come true.[3] Even today, in the midst of hyperbolic and melodramatic Armageddon pitchmen, what you predominantly find is advice on how to master the art of selling... as it worked best in 1997.

Based on our research and field work with clients around the globe, we believe both approaches miss the mark. It's true, selling like it's 1997 (or even 2017) doesn't work like it used to. If traditional consultative selling isn't as effective anymore, then working on ways to implement it is akin, as they say, to rearranging deck chairs on the Titanic.

So, throw it out and start over, right? The sky is falling. Frogs. Armageddon! Well, not so fast. We researched it, and that's not what we found. But doing the same thing as before won't work either. Consultative selling itself has evolved.

Evolve or Perish

Evolving buying trends and rapidly changing technologies are threatening many sales jobs.

Forrester Research predicted in 2015 that 4.5 million business-to-business sales jobs in the U.S. would fall by a million by 2020, a 22 percent reduction.[4]

In the ensuing five years we didn't see that happen. But the research is still largely on target. Here's how.

The researchers placed sellers into four categories (see Figure 2.1). The first three were sellers they labeled as Order Takers, Explainers, and Navigators. These were all job-loss candidates. To different degrees, they would all lose out to 1) technology that facilitates purchasing and 2) massive amounts of information available to buyers broadly on the internet.

The fourth category, Consultants, they said, "explain abstract concepts, solution sell, and build relationships." They were described as "true consultants," and researchers expected job growth in the category.

They were wrong about the job loss numbers, but conceptually they were on track, based on what we have observed working with hundreds of organizations around the globe and through the RAIN Group Center for Sales Research. There were no net job losses overall. However, the Order Takers, Explainers, and Navigators are, in fact, failing predictably. They get hired, they apply the wrong (or no) skills to their work, and because they underperform, they lose their jobs. Companies react, and they retool but not in the right ways, and they hire the same type of seller again. And fail again. Economic stress such as occurred in 2020 has, for some companies, broken this cycle. Companies letting sales people go are reevaluating who the real keepers are.

Now more than ever, as buying and selling dynamics continue to rapidly change, only a special new type of consultative seller will thrive regardless of the medium, and regardless of the economic picture.

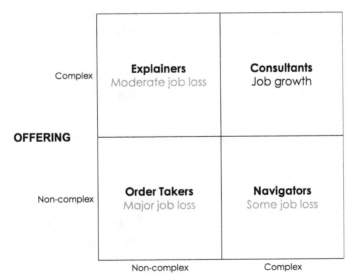

FIGURE 2.1   Death of a B2B Salesman

We believe, whether through face-to-face or virtual selling, that Consultants (or consultative sellers as we redefine the role in the coming pages) will see significant job growth because of the value they add for the buyer.

What, then, do these sellers do to add said value?

What Sales Winners Do Differently

While many sellers are running their old playbooks and losing sales they used to win, others are winning and winning consistently. We wanted to know why, so we posed the question: "What are the winners of actual sales opportunities doing differently than the sellers who come in second place?"

To find the answer, the RAIN Group Center for Sales Research analyzed more than 700 business-to-business purchases made by a broad sample of buyers responsible for $3.1 billion in annual purchasing power.

Here are some key findings, summarized from our book, *Insight Selling*:

- Winners sell radically differently than second-place finishers. In many ways, what sales winners do differently is both surprising and fascinating.
- There's a specific combination of behaviors that sales winners do and outcomes they achieve that second-place finishers don't.
- Several key factors that set winners apart are rarely discussed in the world of selling. They now demand attention.
- Consultative (or solution) selling is not dead, but fundamental consultative sales concepts require reimagining and relabeling if it is to be successful. While traditional or core consultative selling concepts are necessary, they're no longer sufficient to win sales.

What does this all mean? A new future for consultative selling has arrived.

Putting the Consulting in Consultative Selling

Think for a minute about the consulting industry. Strategy firms like Bain, McKinsey, Roland Berger, Boston Consulting Group, and Booz Allen help their clients make the best decisions to drive their success.

These strategy consulting firms redefine reality for their clients using two common strategies:

1. **Give Advice:** Sometimes they do it evangelically, such as sharing with clients the direction an industry is going or how a new technology is emerging, and then providing ideas for how to take advantage. Sometimes they do it after collaborative analysis: They study and interact with clients to dig deep into their situations and needs, and then provide guidance for what to do next. They give advice that inspires their clients and drives them to new heights.

2. **Question the Status Quo:** Strategy consultants push back. They don't accept current thinking and paradigms. Always leery of the dangers in the comfort zone, these consultants challenge everything about the status quo. The end result is rigorous analysis and critical thinking leading to aha moments that shape decision making.

Both traits of strategy consultants lead to the same outcome for their clients: They redefine reality.

Peter Block, author of *Flawless Consulting*, would call these consultants "collaborators." Collaborators, he says, don't just create and implement solutions, they give clients fresh perspectives. Clients, Block says, benefit from their diversity of experience, and work with consultants to define the problem before solving anything.

Another type of consultant is one Block would call a "pair of hands." Their job is to understand the need as presented by the client, position their offerings to solve the need, and execute.

Pair of hands consultants do not redefine reality. They may execute effectively (no small feat), and perhaps have their own novel ways of doing so, but the client's reality stays the same.

Exploring the dynamics of consulting itself is instructive because these dynamics parallel, almost exactly, what's happening with consultative selling.

- Consultative selling *has been defined* for half a century like pair of hands consulting: understand need as defined by the buyer, present offerings as solutions, execute.
- Consultative selling *will be defined* to include strategy consulting: anticipate need, anticipate eventualities, provide and inspire new ideas, challenge the status quo, drive change, drive decision-making, redefine reality.

After almost fifty years of consultative selling focusing on implementation of the buyer's vision, the concept breaks new ground to include strategy consulting where the seller takes an active role in setting, or later, altering and improving the agenda itself. Consultative sellers would do well to think about themselves less as consultative sellers and more like actual strategy consultants. In doing so, it will be easier to shed old thinking about what a consultative seller "is" and "should do," and embrace a new self-image that includes strategy defining, as well as understanding and executing.

This is more of an evolution than a revolution, but it will require a new approach and advanced skill set that many sellers don't have. We call this type of advanced consultative selling Insight Selling.

Consultative Selling—A New Definition

We propose the following new definition for consultative selling:

Consultative selling is an approach to sales whereby sellers redefine reality and maximize buyer value through:

- Understanding, shaping, and redefining need; crafting compelling solutions to address the need; communicating maximum impact for the buyer (core consultative selling)
- Inspiring buyers and driving change with ideas that matter (advanced consultative/ Insight Selling)

As a result of these actions, consultative sellers build relationships, build trust with buyers, and maximize sales wins. Some of the first part of this definition is similar to the traditional definition for consultative selling shared earlier. Sellers are still required to understand need and craft compelling solutions. But as we found in our *What Sales Winners Do Differently* research, this is now often just the price of entry.[5] The sellers who win today, and will win tomorrow, take it a step further. When analyzing what most separated sales winners from second-place finishers, we considered forty-two factors from the buyer's perspective.

The top three factors that most separated winners from second-place finishers were:

1. Educated me with new ideas and perspectives
2. Collaborated with me
3. Persuaded me we would achieve results

This research data underscores the evolution sellers must make. They have to educate (inspire buyers, ideas that matter), they have to collaborate (redefine need, redefine reality, drive change), and persuade buyers they will achieve results (compelling solutions, communicate impact, ideas that matter, build trust).

None of these are easy to do virtually, but for those sellers who take the lead and become Insight Sellers, virtualizing these skills will only serve to differentiate them more.

Selling in the Blue Ocean

W. Chan Kim and Renee Mauborgne, the authors of *Blue Ocean Strategy*, one of the most popular business books in recent memory, argue that companies "succeed not by battling competitors, but rather by creating 'blue oceans' of uncontested market space. They assert that these strategic moves create a leap in value for the company, its buyers, and its employees while making the competition irrelevant."[5,6]

This is exactly what Insight Sellers do. At first, many sales look like Figure 2.2 below.

When the buyer states a need and several competitors try to solve it (core consultative selling), sellers get stuck in a capabilities battle. Since buyers largely perceive vendors to have somewhat interchangeable capabilities, price pressure and low win rates rule the day.[7]

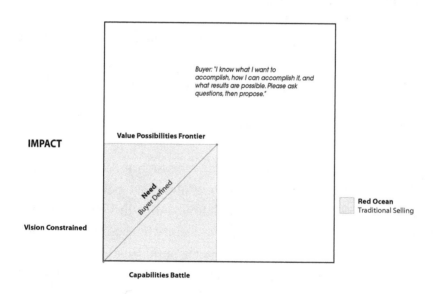

FIGURE 2.2 Value Possibilities Frontier

When sellers educate with new ideas that inspire buyers and question a buyer's status quo, several things happen:

- Sellers redefine the need
- Buyer perception of value they can realize is expanded by the seller; the seller maximizes the impact potential
- Other sellers continue to fight over the originally stated need; the Insight Seller is selling a significantly different solution to a changed buyer perception of need

The net effect is the seller creates a surge in value for the buyer while making themselves categorically distinct from the competition (or sui generis), thus making the leap from the red ocean to the blue ocean.

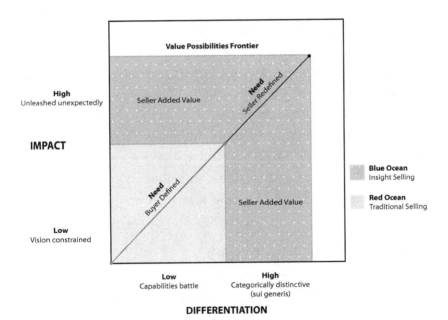

FIGURE 2.3 Blue Ocean Selling

Tyranny of the "OR," Genius of the "AND"

You might be saying to yourself, "I have always asked questions to uncover need, positioned my offerings and solutions, and have won. It doesn't feel like red ocean to me."

Indeed, consultative selling using this framework has been successful for decades. Doing it well is still helpful and necessary to win. Sometimes it's enough by itself, but that's occurring less often now, and we predict even less often in the future.

The problem is when everyone else is doing it too. (Bully for you if your competitors still aren't, but this is true of a smaller and smaller pool of sellers.) If your competitors are also good at core consultative selling, and the offering sets are similar, it's difficult to differentiate.

However, if you practice core consultative selling and provide ideas that change buyer thinking, open up new value possibilities, and change their thinking paradigms, you help them make better decisions. They'll make a stronger impact and create better results, and so will you: You'll find yourself in the winner's circle more often and with less price pressure.

As Jim Collins and Jerry Porras, authors of *Built to Last* would say, it's not "OR," it's "AND."[8] You don't have to make a choice to practice core or advanced consultative selling in general. Success requires using both and choosing which to apply as situations warrant.

Value and the Five Cases

One of the most striking findings from our *What Sales Winners Do Differently* research was that only one factor of the forty-two we studied met the following six criteria:

1. It was something more sales winners did at a high frequency overall.
2. It was something sales winners did most differently than second-place finishers.

3. It was something buyers reported that second-place finishers should change.
4. It drove buyer satisfaction with the buying process.
5. It drove buyer likelihood to buy again.
6. It drove buyer likelihood to refer the seller to their colleagues and peers.

That one factor was, "Overall value from the company is superior to other options." So, it was not about product and service differentiation. It was a factor related to the seller—the overall value—that made the most difference.

What, then, does value actually mean? How do we break that down so we can be the sellers that have buyers saying the "overall value is superior" to other options?

Imagine it's the end of a long, important sales process. Your buyer has given you the verbal "yes" to buy, but he has to deliver a summary of the value proposition case—why he's made the decision to move forward with you—to his peers and the board of directors. And no, you can't attend the meeting to speak alongside him. He must make the argument himself, and it has to be good.

Every argument like this ever made has three essential components that make up the value proposition. The buyer must be able to make a persuasive and compelling case for:

1. Why they want and need what you're selling—what resonates with them.
2. Why you stand out as the best choice from the other available options—what differentiates you.
3. Why they believe that you will deliver on your promises—what substantiates their belief in you.

Here's what happens, however, if one of the components is missing:

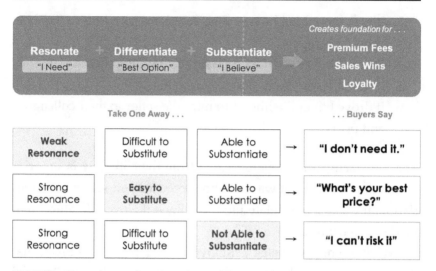

FIGURE 2.4 Three Components of the Value Proposition: Resonate, Differentiate, Substantiate

Take any one of these components away and selling becomes much more difficult.

- If you don't resonate with the buyer, they won't believe that your solution is important enough to feel motivated to buy, or urgent enough to act quickly.
- If you don't differentiate, there's no clear case you are the best choice. Thus, buyers will pressure you on price or turn to a competitor.
- If you don't substantiate with solid proof of your abilities, buyers won't believe you'll follow through on your promises or achieve intended results. They won't risk working with you.

Your actual value proposition—the collection of reasons people buy from you—may share some themes but it will be different from one buyer to the next. In fact, that's what you want: a value case designed specifically for each buyer. That's when you win more than your fair share, because it's likely your competitors aren't this focused on specific value.

The Five Cases

There are five cases sellers must make to ensure the value proposition for each buyer is as strong as it can be. As you read on beyond this chapter, keep in mind these specific principles are strategic components to virtual selling, as they are the keystone to a successful insight selling approach, done virtually.

1. **Priorities:** Sellers need to make sure that buyers choose the right top-of-agenda priorities. Think making sure buyers know they should *"Do this, not that."*

2. **Approaches:** Once buyers choose the right priorities, they need to tackle them the right way. Think making sure buyers know they should *"... this way, not that."*

3. **Return on Investment:** Sellers need to make the case for impact, as impact drives buyer urgency and action. Impact is emotional and rational. Think making sure buyers believe in the most powerful reasons, or *"... because."*

4. **Decisions:** Buyers must then act. They need to know what to do next and when. Think making sure buyers believe in the path. In other words, *"Act now, not later."*

5. **Partners:** Finally, once buyers plan to act (do this) in a certain way (this way) with urgency (because) following a certain path (take action) they need to choose their partner to do it with them. Thus, finishing the flow *"... with us, not them."*

   Do this, not that... this way, not that... because. Act now, not later... with us, not them.

The first two cases, priorities and approaches, are the reasons we spent so much effort earlier in this chapter outlining how consultants drive buyer changes in thinking, and how they bring new and different approaches to the table to solve challenges. Sellers need to do the *exact same thing* to succeed. When they do, they literally become the value that buyers are buying, and become vital to buyer success. On the flip side, when sellers don't make a significant effort, well, remember the job-loss plight of Order Takers, Navigators, and Explainers.

The third case, ROI, isn't a new topic, but sellers remain particularly challenged when selling virtually at building and communicating the return on investment case. Especially in challenging economic environments, making the ROI case is vital to success.

The fourth case, decisions, is about getting buyers to act. In any selling environment this can be an uphill battle. If you are selling during an economic downturn it becomes even harder.

Finally, in the fifth case, building relationships and differentiating are much more difficult in a virtual environment.

If you can make the first three cases really well, you have a huge advantage over those who don't. Since many don't, it's a good argument for making sure you are the one that can.

Throughout this book we'll focus on helping you make all five cases. For now, know that when you make them your value proposition case will be rock solid, and you'll put yourself in a winning position time after time.

The Opportunity Ahead

Much to the chagrin of the oracles of Armageddon, consultative selling—even in its core form—is here to stay.

However, sellers who win go beyond core consultative selling. They are Insight Sellers, able to make five cases to inspire buyers with new ideas and perspectives, and influence how they tackle their priority initiatives. They question the status quo, and don't let buyers accept it, thus redefining reality, whether they meet with buyers to do it in person or virtually.

Everything noted in this chapter is about *what* sales winners do. The rest of the book is about *how*. Let's get to it.

Chapter 2 Key Takeaways

- **Consultative selling has evolved** and more than ever sellers need to be consultants—able to redefine reality and maximize buyer value through:
  - Understanding, shaping, and redefining need; crafting compelling solutions to address the need; communicating maximum impact for the buyer (core consultative selling).
  - Inspiring buyers and driving change with ideas that matter (advanced consultative/Insight Selling).

- **Our research shows that overall value,** which includes the seller, is the single biggest differentiator in buyer **decision-making**.

- **The ways in which sellers define solutions** for, communicate with, and inspire buyers in a virtual environment largely rests on **case-making,** which are a large focus of this book.

LEADING MASTERFUL VIRTUAL SALES CONVERSATIONS

Purpose, Preparation, and Professionalism

Decision-Maker: "Sorry I'm ten minutes late. I was having trouble logging in. Is everyone on?"

Seller: "Great, glad you're here. Yes, everyone's here. We figured we'd wait for you to get started, as this is your area of leadership. Let's get going. Do you have video?"

Decision-Maker: "Oh, was there supposed to be video? I haven't used this videoconference platform much. Is everyone on video?"

Seller: "Yes, we are now. Just hit the video button."

Decision-Maker: "Okay, did that work?"

Seller: "No, you have to enable your camera first."

Decision-Maker: "Okay, how do I do that?"

Seller: "Start by going into your system folder… "

It's easy enough to start an in-person meeting off on the wrong foot. Selling virtually adds significant complexity, a number of ways to sidetrack the meeting, and the potential to start slowly and lose attention—and never get it back.

While there are similarities between face-to-face and virtual meetings, the character of each are so different that to manage them the same way—from both a communication strategy perspective and technical and tactical perspective—is a recipe for failure.

In an in-person meeting you don't have to do as much to keep buyer's attention. As long as you are not completely bombing the meeting, most buyers will at least keep their focus on you and not, literally, switch to doing something else while they sit right in front of you.

In a virtual meeting, if you fail to engage the buyer and keep it interesting, you may not even notice but the buyer may completely change the channel, so to speak, completely tune you out, and do something else. (More on this later as we discuss the concept of the *engagement threshold*.)

Those sellers, however, who master the medium will gain attention and keep it, where others don't.

While there are many moving parts to leading great virtual sales conversations, a successful strategy boils down to three areas:

1. **Purpose:** If you know what you're trying to achieve, you can orchestrate your sales meetings to help you get there. Too many sales meetings meander aimlessly. This is a mistake many sellers make when selling in person, but through force of personality, some sellers can wing it and get through okay. In virtual selling, you have no room for error.

2. **Preparation:** Preparing for an in-person meeting and for a virtual meeting are similar because they have analogous principles. But in a virtual meeting there's *more to consider*. If you don't prepare the right way for each meeting, many possibilities for failure can crop up.

3. **Professionalism:** This area takes on new meaning in virtual selling. In their interactions, buyers and sellers make judgments: Are you in my league or not? Are you worth my time or not? Should I keep paying attention to you or not? Like preparation, many of the tenets of professionalism are shared

with in-person meetings, but there are others that sellers need to consider to impress buyers virtually.

In this section, we'll focus on both the mechanics of the virtual medium (Chapter 3) and the content of great sales conversations, and teach you how to weave them together to lead masterful virtual sales conversations.

But first, an overview of RAIN.

RAIN—The Structure of Masterful Consultative Sales Conversations Through Any Medium

Research-based Sales Method

In 2005, we undertook a major research effort to discover the underlying structure of the most successful sales conversations. Much of the sales method world was built on platitudes and what was, even at the time, very old research. We wanted to see if up-to-date research would reveal something new, noteworthy, and non-intuitive. In fact, it did.

The result was RAIN—which stands for Rapport, Aspirations and Afflictions, Impact, and New Reality—a simple, memorable, and powerful acronym to help sellers remember, learn, and apply best practices in consultative sales conversations. Now over a million people around the world have been trained on, and achieved significant success by following, RAIN.

Since 2005, we've led a variety of research efforts to learn everything that might be new, and anything that might have changed. We've updated the method with some major revisions, but the acronym RAIN and the concepts that underlie the construct have been validated time and again.

In this book, we cover how to lead masterful *virtual* sales conversations. There's a prequel to that movie, though, and it's this: how to lead masterful sales conversation *in general*.

We'll quickly review the basics. Whether you're new to selling or not, study these concepts as much as anything else. Even if you've been selling for a while, you might just find some helpful nuggets.

The upcoming chapters are organized by first understanding each concept in general, by grasping the dynamics of that concept in face-to-face selling versus virtual selling, and finally applying the concept in virtual selling.

In this brief overview, we focus on using RAIN, in general, to have masterful consultative sales conversations. In the coming chapters, we'll break down each concept in more detail and show you how to bring it alive in the virtual selling world.

RAIN Overview
RAIN stands for:

- Rapport
- Aspirations and Afflictions
- Impact
- New Reality

And the "A" and the "I" perform double duty as a reminder to balance Advocacy and Inquiry, and the "IN" will help you to remember to bring insight to your buyers and maximize your influence.

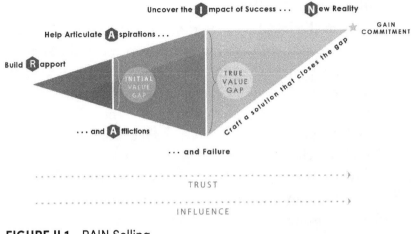

FIGURE II.1   RAIN Selling

The following is an overview of the major components of RAIN.

Rapport

Despite claims in the *Harvard Business Review* that "Selling Is Not About Relationships," our *What Sales Winners Do Differently* research found results to the contrary. The ability to connect with buyers and build strong relationships with them is not only still relevant, it's more important than ever. And while rapport and personal connections don't represent the totality of strong business relationships, they're still very important.

Building rapport is sometimes dismissed as a ploy to make a superficial connection with a potential buyer. We agree—you shouldn't make superficial connections—you should make *genuine* connections. Genuine rapport sets the table for the rest of the conversation and creates the foundation for trust. A genuine connection with a prospect is so important in selling because buyers buy from people they like. Rapport is not enough to win, but without it, you don't get very far.

In Chapter 4 we cover how to build rapport in a virtual setting.

Aspirations and Afflictions

Many sales methodologies suggest that to sell products and services as solutions to needs, you must first uncover the "problem" or "pain." However, these words all too often drive sellers to employ find-out-what's-wrong-and-fix-it thinking. But what if buyers don't think anything's wrong? Soothe-the-pain sellers find themselves at a dead end. No problems to fix means nothing to sell.

The sellers who are most successful at creating opportunities also focus on the positives—goals, aspirations, and possibilities achievable by the buyer, even if the buyer doesn't know it yet. Sellers who focus on aspirations as well as afflictions are able to directly influence the buyer's agenda—and drive their own demand—by inspiring buyers with possibilities they hadn't been considering, but should be.

Think of aspirations **as much as** afflictions in your needs discovery process, and you will remember to ask future-seeking as well as problem-solving questions—questions with themes like "Where do you want to go?" and "What are the possibilities?"

In Chapter 5 we cover how to lead a thorough and powerful discovery of Aspirations and Afflictions in a virtual setting.

Impact

After you uncover a prospect's Aspirations and Afflictions, the questions become, "So what? If your afflictions don't get solved, so what? What won't happen? Will they get worse? How will they affect the bottom line of your company, division, or department? How will they affect your life?"

And:

"If your aspirations don't become reality, so what? Will your competition get ahead of you if you don't innovate? Will you lose market share if you aren't aggressive in your strategy? Will you never be able to grow your business to a point where you can sell it and reach your personal financial goals? Will the promotion you desire continue to elude you?"

The exact "so what" questions will vary depending on the situation, but your ability to quantify and paint the "so what" picture is the foundation for how important it is for the decision-maker to buy from you. The more impact, the more urgency to buy.

In Chapter 6 we discuss how to craft and communicate ROI and overall impact in virtual selling.

New Reality

One of the greatest difficulties in sales is helping prospects understand exactly what they get when they work with you. For that to happen, you must:

- **Establish the New Reality Benchmark:** At the end of a well-managed sales process, you need buyers to see that where they are now is not good enough, because there's a much better place they can be. That is the new reality. They may have an idea of what that new reality is, or you may have to show them what's possible. The point is to put a finish line in their sights, or they'll never get out of the gate.

- **Quantify the Impact:** Will they save 22 percent or $1.2 million on costs of widgets? Improve their cycle times by thirteen days? Improve quality levels by 17 percent? Quantifying the new reality makes buyers pay attention, and gives them justification (for themselves and for others) for moving forward.

- **Paint the Before-and-After Picture:** If "a picture is worth a thousand words," then a graphic that juxtaposes the current state and the new reality is worth even more. The goal is to paint a *compelling* picture. Doing so will show that it's in their interest to take action, increase the perceived and emotional value of making a change, and demonstrate that you are the best choice to help.

A seller's job is to drive change. When you paint a powerful picture of what will be different for the buyer, you make a compelling case for change.

In Chapter 7 we show how to craft and communicate new reality in virtual selling, especially through the structure of a Buyer Change Blueprint℠ graphic.

Advocacy and Inquiry

The "A" and the "I" also help us remember to balance Advocacy and Inquiry.

Many inexperienced sellers believe their job is to show and tell. And tell. And tell. Incessant pitching and presenting feels to buyers like they're being pushed. If you're doing all the talking, they'll feel like you are self-centered, don't care about them, and don't understand their situations and needs (even if you do). Worst of all, savvy buyers will peg you as an amateur and dismiss you. People like to talk about themselves and tell their own stories. Make sure you give your buyers this opportunity.

Salespeople are often told, at some point in their careers, "The sellers who succeed the most always ask great questions." This is true to a point; asking incisive questions is critical to sales success, but some sellers take the advice too literally. If they always ask questions, they don't share a point of view or an opinion, don't tell stories, and don't help set the agenda for success. Although questions can be quite valuable, there's a fine line between being interested and sounding like you're interrogating the buyer. Buyers need to know what you bring to the table. You may ask good questions, but buyers need to know what you're selling them in terms of offerings and outcomes. The key is to balance Advocacy and Inquiry, and to learn when to use one or the other.

Throughout *Virtual Selling* we cover a variety of questions you can ask throughout the selling process. In Chapters 8 and 9 we cover the core framework for telling a persuasive story, and using that framework to present a proposal.

Insight and Influence

Sales is about change. Sellers must be influence masters to be successful in selling. The "IN" in RAIN is a reminder to be a master of influence, including inspiring your buyers with insight. Master the principles of Insight Selling, and you'll become more influential and effective in each stage of your sales conversations.

In Chapters 8 and 9 we consider how to craft and communicate a Convincing Story to inspire buyers with ideas (i.e., deliver a compelling persuasive presentation), and in Chapter 10 we discuss how to lead virtual collaboration sessions.

The RAIN Selling model works because when you use it you'll be selling like sales winners do. And you'll be doing what most buyers say virtual sellers don't do, but should.

With RAIN, if you take the key principles to heart, you can use it right away. It's simple like that. Yet it's rich and sophisticated enough that, with study and practice, continuing to get better at the core components will help you continue to improve your results. If you're new to the RAIN model of consultative selling, in the pages that follow you'll be introduced to the key concepts, with a special focus on applying it in virtual selling. But as far as general concepts go, we'll be keeping it short in order to focus on the virtual selling specifics.

For those of you who want to dive in deeper into the techniques for leading powerful sales conversations, read our books *Rainmaking Conversations* and *Insight Selling*, visit the book tools (http://raingrp.com/VS-BookTools) with *Virtual Selling*, and visit www.raingroup.com to explore various training options for individuals and teams at mid-size and large organizations.

CHAPTER 3

MASTERING THE MEDIUM: VIRTUAL MEETING MECHANICS, SETUP, AND TECHNOLOGY

> To learn more about RAIN Selling, visit the *Virtual Selling* book tools on the RAIN Group website for free content (http://raingrp. com/VS-BookTools), or pick up a copy of the *Wall Street Journal* bestselling book, *Rainmaking Conversations*.

The Engagement Threshold

Meeting mechanics and technology are tactical areas. If you do the dos, and avoid the don'ts, you will be in a position to lead great virtual sales meetings. This chapter will help you avoid the technical and mechanical hiccups that can derail a virtual meeting.

But before we get to the dos and don'ts, we need to introduce you to a concept that will have a significant impact on your virtual selling success.

If you're in a live sales meeting in a conference room, it's unlikely that a buyer will, while you're talking, pull out their phone and start responding to text and email messages, check the news, or start fiddling on social media. But they do in virtual meetings. A lot. In fact, 92 percent of people admit to multitasking during meetings.[1]

Consider just how much more difficult it is to pay attention in virtual meetings. According to researchers at the University of

Toronto, York University, and SUNY Albany, 94.4 percent of meeting participants say they are able to pay attention during face-to-face meetings, but in the virtual world it drops to 41.7 percent.[2]

And a recent *Harvard Business Review (HBR)* article said, "Attendees often interpret virtual meetings as a license to multi-task."[3]

Why is it so difficult to maintain attention during virtual meetings?

- **Maintaining Gaze:** It's very tiring to look people in the eye, and focus attention on their faces, for long periods. This doesn't happen in live meetings, but it's all we have in virtual ones.

- **Baseline Stress:** Given that people are often generally stressed out, their energy tanks aren't necessarily full when your meeting starts. And if your meeting is the sixth one in a row, energy can be further depressed.

- **Compulsive Task Switching:** Most people are rapid task switchers, especially while they are at their computers. As noted in *HBR*, people view virtual meetings as a license to multi-task.

- **Ringelmann Effect:** The Ringelmann effect states that the more people involved in a task, the less effort they devote to it individually. Thus, the more people you have in a virtual meeting, the less likely they are to be engaged.

It's up to the seller, then, to take the lead to minimize multitasking by maximizing buyer engagement during virtual meetings. Throughout *Virtual Selling* we discuss ways to maximize virtual meeting engagement. Here we give an overview of the concept of why it's so difficult and summarize ways to make sure you maintain the engagement threshold.

The engagement threshold is simply this: The point at which attention is captured and maintained, and below which attention is lost.

> **ENGAGEMENT THRESHOLD**
>
> The point at which attention is captured and maintained, and below which attention is lost.

Let's say you have a thirty-minute meeting. If you ran the meeting virtually the same way you would run it live, it's possible you might not reach what is a higher engagement threshold.

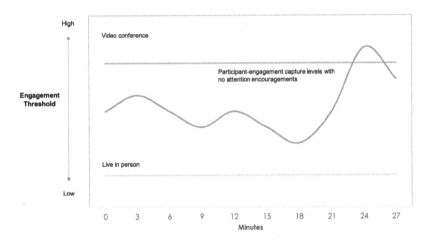

FIGURE 3.1 Engagement Threshold with No Attention Encouragements

It's not even quite that simple, though. Because of the Ringelmann effect, the more people at a meeting, the more likely they are to tune out. In virtual meetings, because it's easier to hide, the more people the faster the engagement threshold rises.

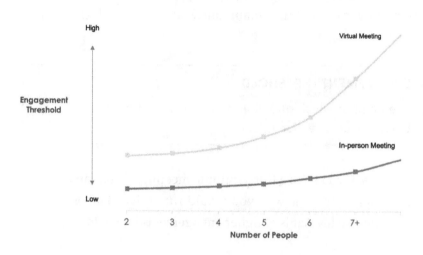

FIGURE 3.2 Engagement Threshold with Increasing Number of People

Achieving the Engagement Threshold

The secret to achieving and maintaining buyer engagement, we've found, is to use the 30 + 3 rule. A seller (or anyone running a virtual meeting) has thirty seconds to grab (or lose) engagement. And because the medium makes it so easy for participants to lose focus, sellers need to *re-achieve* engagement every three minutes.

While you'll find ideas for achieving and maintaining engagement throughout this book, here's a summary of the key ways to do it.

BEFORE THE CALL

Prepare to use the following:

- Build in structural engagement such as virtual whiteboarding, screen sharing, and poll taking.
- Create intrigue and build anticipation levels, such as through setting up meeting topics and reveals (e.g., In a few minutes,

I'll share the three keys our research has shown to maximize your success in «fill in the blank».)

- Raise your visual asset game. Employ frequent, purposeful screen and slide motion such as in building Buyer Change Blueprints (Chapter 7) and Convincing Stories (Chapter 8).
- Schedule meetings on the 15s and 45s to give buyers mental breaks from meetings that tend to end on the 00s and the 30s.
- Schedule meetings earlier in the day to avoid being the sixth virtual meeting in a row the buyer attends.

DURING THE CALL

- Open strong with immediate interaction.
- Tell frequent, brief stories (stories of any sort are very engaging).
- Talk about the buyers since people tend to find themselves quite interesting.
- Keep any delivery or talking to three minutes; fix minutes maximum before asking a question or stopping for an interaction.
- Make attention an imperative; call people by name. Ask them a question. Ask for an interaction. For example, you might say, "Beth, I'm curious to know your reaction to that." Be emotionally intelligent about calling on people, but as you use their names, it'll put everyone on notice that their attention is important.

And, finally, to the extent that you can, minimize the number of attendees to reduce the Ringelmann effect and keep the engagement threshold as low as it can be. Of course, it's best to have the right decision-makers and influencers present, but if the meeting gets too big, it'll be that much more difficult to keep everyone engaged.

Seven Areas for Focus

Now that you're aware of the engagement threshold you must achieve (and we'll cover ways throughout *Virtual Selling* to achieve the highest level of engagement), let's dig into meeting mechanics. Getting the basic mechanics right will get you started off on the right foot.

Here are seven technical and tactical areas that sellers need to attend to in virtual selling that are quite different than in face-to-face selling:

1. Conversation Setup
2. Platform
3. Video
4. Audio
5. Lighting
6. Background
7. You

These areas are not all mutually exclusive. Some setup crosses over to video and platform. Some video and audio crosses over to you, and so on. The idea, however, is that sellers who attend to all seven will create a clean, professional presentation and stand apart from those who don't.

Before we dive in, a thought for those of you who are not technically or visually inclined: get help. Ask for help. Pay for help. Do whatever you need—just get help. To the extent you don't, buyers will notice you grappling with technical blips, lose trust and doubt your efficacy and knowledge in general.

1. Conversation Setup

- *Bandwidth:* Make sure you have enough coming to your home or office to have stable video and audio. Every system and location have different needs. To find out yours, start by Googling the bandwidth you need and make sure you have enough coming in. The best check, however, is to ask people you know (i.e., colleagues, not buyers) to sit in on a short mock session and let you know if any video or audio issues arise, and tackle any challenges from there.

- *Technical setup and links:*
  - Make sure URL links in meeting notices are clear to participants for logging in.
  - Outline the agenda in the meeting notice and use a clear meeting title (some platforms auto-name meetings, you should rename them).
  - Use one-touch dialing features so people dialing in on cell phones don't have to stop and type.
  - Use meeting auto-reminders for the day before the meeting is scheduled. Many online appointment-setting software programs have this feature. Autoresponder systems can be set up to send emails at a specific time, or simply remind people.
  - If there are any technical needs—such as downloading, security management, or technical configuration before the meeting—organize and communicate pre-meeting tasks. Create a standing notice that if a buyer is joining on a tablet or mobile device to download any needed apps beforehand.
  - Create a calendar invitation and send; when you get an acceptance, you know you made it through any spam filters.
  - Make sure time zones are correct in meeting notices; hard-type meeting times if meetings cross time zones so people don't get confused.
  - Set up any security beforehand and make it clear, such as if there's a password and how to log in.
- *Pre-meeting:* Check your video, bandwidth, audio, webcam, office scene, lighting. Get your screens and files ready.

You don't need tech check prior to every meeting, but if a meeting is very important, double checking will save you heartaches.

- *Recording permission:* If you are going to record the meeting, make sure you say it out loud and get your attendees' confirmation—before you record.

- *Sharing the recording:* It's a good idea to share the recording with buyers. You never know when they will watch it again or share it. If you want to be impressive:
  - *Edit:* Whether yourself, someone on your team or a service, you can edit the meeting so dead air and slow moments are removed. A clean, edited version of the meeting is very impressive to buyers. Don't do this often, but do it if you think a meeting is really worth it, or if the recording might get forwarded to other decision-makers.
  - *Playback speed:* Explain to buyers when you share the recording how to play it back at faster speeds. For example, on a Mac with Quicktime, if you hold the option button and press the fast-forward button, it incrementally speeds up playback.

FIGURE 3.3   Playback Speed

2. Platform

- *Selection:* If you have the choice, it's typically best to select a meeting software that most people are used to. Ease-of-use for buyers should be your #1 criteria. Which one you select will depend on your individual needs, but don't pick one that will make it difficult for buyers to figure out how to use. Simplest for buyers is best.

- *Your place or mine:* Use your platform for meetings, if at all possible. It makes for fewer technical snafus on your part.

- *Screen-share hygiene:* When sharing screens:
  - Have an appropriately professional background screen.
  - Clean up your desktop files. Having a thousand folders or files named, "Jones Negotiation: Confidential," "Catching up to my quota," or "How «our competitor» is crushing it" are all bad form.
  - Turn off screen pop-ups. Nobody wants to see your emails pop in. During the entire meeting. Non-stop. As you click them off, one by annoying one.
  - Close browsers and any personal files. "10 Instant Pot Recipes Grammie Will Love" is not something decision-makers will love.

- *Plan B:* Sometimes meeting software platforms don't work. Have a plan B and be ready to set it up in real time. Practice setting up on another platform in 60 seconds.

PLATFORM FLEXIBILITY

We at RAIN Group have clients who expect the use of different platforms for their meetings. You might want to use your platform, but be ready to use theirs. Become familiar with how to use each, have the technology ready on your computer in advance, and test it. Over the course of just a few weeks, we attended meetings on Zoom, Webex, Microsoft Teams, GoToMeeting, BlueJeans, and Skype. If you don't have your video (and audio) prepared, you run the risk of wasting valuable meeting time getting set up, and frustrating your buyers in the process.

---

3. Video

- *Turn your video on:* It's a best practice to use video for your virtual sales meetings. Even if the buyer doesn't have their video on, seeing your face on the screen will help develop trust and rapport.

- *Set expectations in advance to use video:* Prepare for video on every call, and communicate this in advance to set expectations with your buyer. Write explicitly in your meeting invitation, "I'll have webcam video on for this call. Here's how to turn yours on and check in advance." That way, you minimize the risk of having people not feeling "camera ready" when it comes time for the meeting. Notice we didn't say, "We'll be using video for this call." That could turn off a buyer who doesn't like video. But if you say, "I'll have mine on," there's no heavy handedness, and they'll get the idea just the same.

- *Use an HD webcam:* Most computers these days have webcams, but they are not typically very good. People who don't use an HD webcam are often grainy on video, and poor lighting conditions make it even worse.

  Your webcam affects your appearance. If you have a grainy webcam, it's like wearing crumply clothes to a meeting. You wouldn't do that, and HD webcams cost less than a suit.

- *Head position:* Be aware of where your head is. Don't be the person whose chin or forehead is cut off. There's one in every meeting. The top of your head should be 10 percent to 15 percent from the top of your screen.

- *Look into the camera:* Don't look left or right. This is distracting. Don't look off to a second monitor for long periods. Look directly into the camera. If you're typing notes or need to see something, put it on your main screen, right under your camera, and you solve this problem.

- *Position the camera at eye level or just above:* Avoid acute angles with your camera position. Anyone who's a seasoned selfie-taker knows to position the camera at eye level or slightly above.

| Camera too high | Camera too low |

FIGURE 3.4   Video Adjustments

- *Stay in the visual:* Don't turn your video on and off, and as a rule don't get up and walk around. If you need to turn the video off, do so as infrequently as possible for as short periods as possible.

4. Audio

"Can you hear me now?"

"I'm getting feedback. Who has their phone and computer audio on?"

"Move closer to your microphone… "

"You're on mute!"

All too familiar, all worth avoiding.

- *Get a high-quality microphone:* Computer microphones aren't typically very good. Invest in an external mic or quality headset. Also consider your background noise. Some microphones are good at picking up voice only and leaving off ambient sound. There are plenty of excellent options.

- *Dial in if needed:* When bandwidth or audio quality are issues, dial in on the phone. Make sure you have a strong cell signal, or use a landline. If you dial in, get a high-quality Bluetooth headset. If you use typical wired earbuds, the mic can scratch against you and sound annoying on the other end.

- *Test sound:* Prior to meetings, do a tech check to test your audio. It's all too common that people buy and plug in a high-quality external mic, then forget to enable it!

- *Turn off notifications:* This is a big one. One of the most common, loud, and jarring annoyances for buyers is when seller notifications keep dinging loudly. This includes email, meeting notifications, Slack messages, text messages, phone ringers, and screen pop-ups. These alerts and noises are distracting, and they bother your buyers. Turn them off.
  - *Minimize background noises:* Barking, voices, lawnmowers, etc. To the extent you can, minimize these external noises. A high-quality mic with noise-cancelling features can also help. If you need everyday noise reduction, you can get acoustic foam panels or other inexpensive home soundproofing systems, or consider soundproofing your office if the problem is significant and long term.
  - *Mute typing noises:* It's okay to type and take notes during your sales calls, but when you do so, mute yourself or get a quiet keyboard. Loud typing noises are incredibly distracting.
  - *Use mute wisely, stay aware:* If you do put yourself on mute while typing, or if there's a lot of noise, make sure to unmute yourself when it's time to speak. You want to avoid having to say, "Sorry, I was on mute."

5. Lighting

Lighting issues abound when it comes to video meetings. It's not that difficult to control light. You don't need a degree in lighting. Usually all that's needed is playing around with it for fifteen minutes. Here are our top tips.

- *Face lighting:* Light evenly, with medium-to-light brightness. You often need lighting to be brighter than you think. If you've ever done a professional video, news interview, or photo shoot, you're familiar with the bright lights that are used.

Lighting is too dark   Lighting is too bright

FIGURE 3.5 Lighting Adjustments

- *Shine:* If you've ever done a video shoot, you know all professional videographers will pat your head and face with powder to decrease shine. Consider it if you're on the shiny side.

- *Backlighting and overheads:* Backlighting creates dark faces and shadows. Overhead lights often create glare. Test your lighting. Be mindful to reduce both.

- *Purpose-built camera lights:* Use purpose-built video and photography lighting, desk lights, and dimmers as needed and as lighting conditions change. I (Mike) live on a lake and sit with the view of the lake behind me. This creates an incredible amount of backlight, making me look like I'm in witness protection. I use ring lights to brighten my face and it works fine. The shine on the lights, however, appeared in the windows! (This can also show up as a reflection in eyeglasses.) So I moved lighting positions to compensate.

- *Pay attention to time of day:* Where I sit, in the morning the sun is right behind me. For the mornings, I have a green screen. Takes fifteen seconds to stand it up before calls. During the day I use the ring lights. In the winter, when the light gets low late afternoon, I have to be prepared to switch lighting in real time because it goes from sunny to dark quickly. It doesn't take much more than awareness and forethought to keep up.
  - *Color temperature adjustment*: Depending on the light in your room and time of day, you can look somewhere between blue and orange. Use color temperature adjustments for hue control. Stay more white/blue than orange.

6. Background

Your background makes a strong statement about you and it's a big part of your brand. Many people don't notice this one until it's pointed out to them, usually because they need to change something. It's rarer, but much more preferable to have someone say, "Wow, I love your background." Here are tips on having a great background:

- *Four core options:* The first is best. The others can also be solid:
  - Prepared actual background settings that are neat, clean, bright, and professional
  - Green screen with virtual background (avoid goofier-side backgrounds such as outer space and the Golden Gate Bridge)
  - Step-and-repeat banner-style background (see further explanation below)

- ○ Plain, preferably monochromatic wall with or without windows

- *Setting review:* Carefully review your background for professionalism. Clean your bookshelf. Remove boxes and trash. De-clutter the area. Prepared home backgrounds are all okay if meticulously curated. I was on a call recently and there was a garment rack with suit jackets in the background. It would've been easy for them to roll the clothing rack out of view. Instead, it was there, distracting me the entire meeting. Not as bad as the empty tuna cans, though. You get the idea.

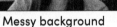

Messy background   Professional, digital background

FIGURE 3.6 Background Adjustments

- *Authenticity:* Real office settings are best and most authentic. Curate your look and scene to project your desired brand.

- *Step and repeat:* A step and repeat is a photo backdrop used for publicity and event photos. Think celebrity pictures at a charity event with the white background covered in logos. You can make one for your company, or really anything. A colleague of ours had one made with his newly published book and company logo. You could do the same thing if you have awards, publications, and so on. Think of a step and repeat as a big poster. If you use a real step and repeat, make sure it's flat (no wrinkles), properly lit, and that you like how you look in front of it. You can also create a virtual step and repeat and use it with a green screen.

- *Motion:* Keep background motion to a minimum. People walking around and other motion in the background is distracting. If you're going to be on a call, set up in an area where there's likely to be little going on behind you, unless it's a really nice setting with little motion, like a calm lake in the background.

- *Green screen:* Use virtual backgrounds with a green screen to create professional-looking backgrounds. Virtual backgrounds without a green screen can look grainy, odd, and sometimes unpleasant; they can also flicker, distracting meeting participants.

7. You

Attend to your own look and project professionalism in your virtual sales meetings.

- *Color contrast:* Make sure your clothes contrast well against the background. Avoid green with green screens. Avoid black with dark backgrounds (or your head will appear to be floating).

- *Think "important live meeting":* Prepare your look and dress as if you were meeting in person. If you're not sure, always dress up one level. Your look is a part of your brand.

Appropriate for velour salespeople

Appropriate for most other salespeople

FIGURE 3.7 "You" Adjustments

- *Avoid busy patterns:* Clothes with busy patterns can look fuzzy on camera and big patterns can be distracting. Lean toward solid colors.

- *Distance:* Remain approximately 1.5 to 2 feet from the camera. You don't want your face to be too small or too big in the scene. Think "TV news anchor" and adjust your distance accordingly.

Too close   Proper distance

FIGURE 3.8   Distance Adjustments

- *Stay present:* This is one of the most important tips in this entire list. Keep your eyes on the camera. Don't check your phone, second screen, or email. Too many sellers find themselves distracted in their sales meetings. Buyers notice. It's a major turnoff.

- *Posture:* Keep good posture. Slouching doesn't look good. Avoid chair rocking and swaying, especially with a chair with a flexible back.

- *Personal animation:* Some sellers overdo animation and facial expressions, which gets distracting. Other sellers don't move at all, which signals disengagement. Balance your animation. Note that most sellers are too understated and should project more.

Chapter 3 Key Takeaways

- **Sellers are change agents.** Masterful sales conversations that build rapport, discover afflictions and aspirations, define impact, and paint a new reality are now largely dependent on sellers who can engage with expertise in a virtual environment.

- **Virtual meeting dynamics** may lead to engagement challenges, with multitasking and fatigue as common outcomes when meeting leaders don't account for engagement thresholds and planful set up.

- **Sellers in a virtual environment** need to gain attention and keep it by focusing on purpose, preparation, and professionalism. Key areas to focus on include:
  - Setup
  - Platform
  - Video
  - Audio
  - Lighting
  - Background
  - You

- Use the checklist in the *Virtual Selling* book tools section of the RAIN Group website (http://raingrp.com/VS-BookTools) to organize, prepare, and improve your virtual setting.

CHAPTER 4

BUILDING RAPPORT AND TRUST IN A 2D WORLD

RAPPORT IS THE *R* IN RAIN SELLING.

To learn more about RAIN Selling, visit the *Virtual Selling* book tools on the RAIN Group website for free content (http://raingrp. com/VS-BookTools), or pick up a copy of the *Wall Street Journal* bestselling book, *Rainmaking Conversations*.

The Role of the Emotional and Rational Brain in Decision-Making

Everybody's brain has two different processing centers: emotional and rational. The emotional brain is old. It developed millions of years ago, first with the raw instincts—like fight or flight—that all animals have, and then into more complex emotions for humans like anger, aggression, desire, fear, hatred, passion, love, disgust, sympathy, and so on.

Then there's the rational side, which developed tens of thousands of years ago. This part of the brain is more deliberate, analyzing and studying, and thinking about the future consequences of various possible actions.

What psychologists know about decision-making is that when the rational and emotional side work together, it's a powerful motivator for action. When the emotional and rational sides are at odds, however, the emotional side typically wins.

The consequences for selling are profound, and it starts with building rapport. The fundamental question of whether someone likes you or doesn't drives a significant portion of how your selling process and the customer's decision process will go.

In our 2020 *Top Virtual Selling Challenges and Priorities* research, 54 percent of buyers told us that when sellers connect with them and build rapport virtually it has a high level of influence on their purchase decision, yet only 25 percent of sellers do this well.

Building rapport leads to some very important outcomes:

- People talk to people they like.
- People share information with people they like.
- People buy from people they like.
- People feel loyalty to people they like.
- People introduce people they like.

In 2019, the RAIN Group Center for Sales Research, surveying a large audience, asked, "What percent of people are trustworthy?"

The most common response? 30 percent.

But when asked, "What percent of people *that you know* are trustworthy?"

The most common response was 70 percent.

Simply being known to someone leads to trust. We all know intuitively how important trust is when selling. While basic familiarity makes a difference in building trust, knowing and liking, well, that's much more powerful, setting the stage for the selling success that comes after.

If you want to build rapport with buyers in a virtual world, you need to succeed with the 4 Principles of Rapport: empathy, authenticity, similarity, and shared experience.

Differences in Rapport-Building: Face-to-Face vs. Virtual Selling

Relationships are a core area where sellers need to take the lead in order to thrive with virtual selling. Let us introduce you to the

Virtual Selling Divergence Scale, a measure of how different a component of selling is when comparing face-to-face vs. virtual selling.

1. Not that much different
2. A little different
3. Somewhat different
4. Different
5. Significantly different

Rapport-building, a key component of relationships, is a **5 out of 5 different**. It's significantly different. Here's how.

Component	Face-to-Face	Virtual Selling
Physical in-room vs. virtual	• Able to read body language	• Barely able to read body language; face only sometimes, and smaller on screen
	• People always in view	• Video may be on, off, or on and off; only face in view
	• More relaxed, feels natural; time feels slower, dead air, and pauses more acceptable	• More business-like feel, time feels quicker, dead air, and pauses less tolerated
Natural flow and space for rapport-building	Able to chat upon entering, walking to room, walking to get coffee, waiting for meeting to start	None of this available naturally in a virtual setting

Component	Face-to-Face	Virtual Selling
Time for personal connection in scheduled meetings	More natural to check in before business agenda; when new people join, everyone stops and shakes hands (pre-pandemic)	Less natural to check in before business agenda; when people join, less natural to stop for introductions; no physical interaction
Small meetings built for rapport-building (e.g., coffee shop)	Commonly set for people to connect for meals, coffee, entertainment events (pre-pandemic)	Not common; dynamics of connection-focused discussions completely changed
Large meetings (e.g., industry events)	Live meetings offer significant, expected short and long rapport-and relationship-building conversations	Rapport and relationship building is difficult in online conferences; warm human interaction is a challenge
Rapport-building around, but not at, meetings	LinkedIn, email, social presence all a part of the picture	LinkedIn, email, and social presence much more powerful and connected parts of the virtual picture

Rapport- and Trust-Building in a Virtual Selling World

No question, trust is essential for selling. If you don't establish rapport, you put trust at risk.

The implication is this: finding ways to build rapport in a virtual world where doing so is difficult is especially important.

> ### RAPPORT LEADS TO TRUST
>
> Trust is a dynamic we all want to achieve in selling (and in life). There are four key components of trust that are important to know.
>
> Rapport is essential for filling the bucket of one of the key trust components—intimacy. The kind of intimacy based on a depth of closeness and affinity. The other components—capability, dependability, integrity—are judgments. Intimacy isn't; it's a feeling.

4 Principles of Rapport

RAIN Group's 4 Principles of Rapport create a solid foundation for strong buyer relationships.

Rapport Principle #1: Cultivate Empathy

Question: What gives your brain as much pleasure as food and money?

Answer: Talking about yourself.

People love to talk about themselves because it feels good. Harvard neuroscientists Diana Tamir and Jason Mitchell conducted a series of behavioral experiments showing that when people disclose information about themselves, the areas of the brain where reward processing takes place are significantly activated.[1]

What this means for you is that if you can get people talking about themselves, you're making progress toward cultivating empathy, and ultimately building rapport. If you can show people you're actually listening to them, they'll be strongly inclined to like you.

For example, you might ask, "How are you managing everything now that you're working from home? What's it like for you to live and work in the same place each day?"

Lead with empathy and listen to how they're doing. You'll learn about kids, pets, and maybe pick up on motivators, or personal goals.

Here are a few other questions you could ask:

- What's going on in your business these days?
- How have things in your business changed given the pandemic and the global economic crisis?
- It was good to hear the short version of your background at the meeting, but since it's just you and me today, I'd love to get the long version. What's your story?
- You mentioned you want to retire in a few years. What are you thinking of doing then? Have the recent economic changes affected your plans?
- Sometimes, sellers say to us, "These questions are pretty basic. What are the more advanced questions here?"

There aren't any. Relationships are pretty straightforward. You don't need to get too fancy to learn about people. Just ask appropriate questions, listen actively, and show that you care.

What you develop is Rapport Principle #1: Empathy. Empathy is the ability to understand and share the feelings of another. If you want to understand another person, get them talking about themselves and demonstrate that you're listening.

---

20 QUESTIONS FOR RAPPORT

Here are 20 questions you can use to build rapport in a virtual setting, in good times and bad.

In general
1. What's going on in your business these days?
2. Do you have any exciting plans for the weekend (last weekend, etc.)?

3. It was good to hear the short version of your background at the meeting, but since it's now just you and me, I'd love to get the long version. What's your story?

4. You mentioned you want to retire in a few years. What are you thinking of doing then?

5. What's a habit of yours that you want to develop or change? (Sometimes it's good to set the tone here with, "I haven't played piano for 20 years, but now again I'm trying to practice piano every day for 20 minutes.")

6. For me, people don't know I am a competitive sailor, and three of my kids are, too. What's something about you that people don't know?

7. Where do you live? What do you love about it?

8. Your company seems like a great place to work—what do you think makes it special?

9. Great to talk today, and glad to be here. But it's 4 p.m., this is my last meeting, and I'm also looking forward to... reading X, cooking Y, watching, Z, playing a game of A, taking a ride to visit B. You?

10. I noticed something interesting on your website about your company doing community work. Can you tell me more?

When times are challenging

11. How have you and your clients been affected since the «the bad news, crisis, economy changed»?

12. Given how everything has changed because of «insert change here», what's one habit of yours that you've changed?

13. What's something you miss that you didn't think you were going to?

14. Is there anything for you, given the changes in «insert here» that turned out better than you expected?

15. How are you taking care of yourself these days? Anything you want to change?

16. How are your friends and family doing?
17. It surprises me how many acts of generosity I've been see-ing. What have you seen?
18. What's giving you hope right now?
19. When everything turns around, what are you looking for-ward to?
20. What's your prediction? How do you think this is all going to pan out?

While most people like a listener, few people like a faker. Anyone who comes across as fake or phony might as well open the other person's brain and press the dislike button.

Rapport Principle #2: Authenticity

Be real.

People like people who are genuine. Research and practice offer many tips on developing authenticity in your interactions.

- Smile slower. Actual research from a study published in the *Journal of Nonverbal Behavior*[2] reveals that when you slow down the onset of a smile (or smile slower), it transmits authenticity to the people with whom you're communicating.
- Don't overdo it. Over-friendliness and saccharin-sweetness often seem like obvious ploys to connect, and people can sense this; they intuitively know when you aren't being authentic.

  You can and should ask the questions noted in the empa-thy section, but if you seem like you're asking just to ask, you'll come across as insincere and it will be self-defeating.

  This is why having a real meeting background when you are on camera is better than a digital, virtual background. It's more authentic. (But, it also has to be professional, so if that's a challenge, go with a nice digital background.)

- Find a similarity with your customer. People like people like them.

Rapport Principle #3: Similarity

The more you can find common ground, the more likely you are to develop genuine rapport.

Various psychological studies show people like names better when they're similar to theirs. They prefer brands when they share their initials. They prefer that people move the way they move.

What can you do to apply the similarity principle?

Find interests and backgrounds in common with the other person and you can make and deepen connections. Anyone who has shared a favorite TV show, sport, author, vacation spot, or other personal nugget knows that these small similarities can bring people together.

When you ask the questions in the empathy section, share similarities. "I have two kids as well, same age as yours! When the crisis hit, home schooling was bananas. One funny thing, kind of like what you said, is that Jimmy, my four year old,... "

Another way to practice the similarity principle is to mirror customers' basic behaviors. If they speak slowly, they likely prefer people who do, too. If they speak quickly, the same. They lean forward, you lean forward. And so on.

The idea here is not to outright mimic, but interact in ways customers like to interact, and interact like them, and you'll develop better connection and rapport.

This is all a little bit more difficult in virtual selling because you really have to tune into the buyer's speaking—words and tone—and their body language on video. Be aware and focus, and you'll be able to demonstrate more similarity

Rapport Principle #4: Shared Experience

Shared experience helps build trust and a sense of camaraderie.

Everyone likes intestinal meat, right? I mean, it's so popular, it's springing up on menus in all the hippest restaurants, and kids are just begging for it.

Well, maybe not, but one psychological experiment involving meat innards showed a surprisingly important aspect of shared experiences.

One of the founders of organizational psychology, Kurt Lewin, created a study in the 1940s with two groups of homemakers. His team lectured the first group about all the reasons for, and benefits of, eating intestinal meats. They also applied social pressure and played on the homemakers' emotions about patriotism ("You'll help the war effort") to persuade them. They even brought in others to talk about how much they loved intestinal meat and gave the homemakers recipes to try.

The second group participated in a facilitated collaborative discussion. Study leaders asked the homemakers about how they might persuade other homemakers to bring the benefits of intestinal meat to their families. They talked it out, role-played conversations, and shared ideas.

The results were astounding:

- 32 percent of the collaborative discussion group went on to serve intestinal meat to their families at home.
- Only 3 percent of the lectured group did.

People who are talked at, or lectured to, don't feel connected or take ownership, resulting in a low level of participation. Whereas people who are involved in a process, who actively interact and collaborate, develop a stronger liking for those who are interacting with them and, at the same time, develop a sense of psychological ownership over whatever they're working on.

What does this mean for you? If you're selling, you can create a shared experience with your buyer by making the process collaborative. For example:

- Define the problem using your buyer's own words.
- Craft a solution alongside your buyer—brainstorming together and co-creating value.

- Devise a strategy to present the solution to the rest of your buyer's team or board.
- Work collaboratively to come to the right agreement and terms.

When you do, they'll not only like you more, but also be more likely to take action on whatever it is you want them to do.

We cover this quite a bit more in Chapter 10, How to Collaborate with Buyers Virtually.

It's also true that if you simply spend time with people—at dinner, coffee, events, and so on—your affinity for one another will rise. But wait! This is—by definition—not possible in virtual selling, which brings us to our next topic on creating the time and space for rapport-building.

Creating Opportunity, Time, and Space for Rapport-Building in Virtual Selling

Below are the critical actions and behaviors that sellers need to do to build rapport virtually.

Deal with physical in-room vs. virtual platform

First, make sure video use is set as an expectation. In Chapter 3 we give advice on messaging about the use of video in meetings. If you can increase your video participation from, say, 71 percent to 93 percent by using good messaging, you will put yourself in a much better position to build rapport.

Second, keep your video on even if the buyer's isn't. Here's what happens:

- Some people are either uncomfortable with video or haven't grown used to it yet but if you are on video, eventually some just turn themselves on, either in that meeting or in a subsequent one. But if you leave yourself off, you don't give this possibility a chance.

- People see you and like you! People respond to faces, not voices alone. Your job is building rapport here. Chapter 3 is dedicated to developing mastery of the medium. Use it to take the lead and engage your buyers with depth.
- Authenticity grows when people see you are a real human being. This is an important victory in virtual selling where everything, by definition, is more impersonal. It's up to you to take the lead and do something to make it more personal.

Natural flow and space for rapport-building; time for personal connections in scheduled meetings

A live meeting at a client's office that starts at 10 a.m. actually starts at 9:40 with arrival. You're then picked up at reception, often by your key contact, then you take the elevator to the right floor and walk to a conference room. As you plug into the projector and wait for others, you chat. All goes well and quickly so you walk to the coffee area and pour a cup with your buyer.

A virtual meeting that starts at 10 a.m. starts at 10 a.m. (Or 10:04 a.m.) Everyone says hello then people jump right into the business at hand.

Importantly, the only exceptions are sellers who take the lead and make space for rapport-building. Let's say you have an hour-long meeting. You don't want to lose the hour to chit chat, but sometimes, after a meeting, we'll have sellers tell us, "I ended up talking to them about life for twenty minutes before we really got to it. We really liked each other, and from a business perspective, we didn't get as far as I wanted, but we're picking it up on a video call on Thursday already."

Don't discount the power of rapport and do give rapport the appropriate amount of time. Ask something like, "Before we get going, let's do a check in; what's going on with everyone?"

For many sellers who do this for the first time, they're surprised by the improved tenor of their meetings.

It's also a temptation to let everyone else go first. But if you want to set the tone, you need to go first. Talk about something hilarious that happened to you over the weekend. Talk about how you're thrilled to play seventy-two holes of golf in three days while the family is away for the long weekend. Whatever you do, people naturally tend to follow with similar commentary. If you want to break the ice a certain way, set the tone and go first.

In face-to-face selling, some of the best conversations happen after the meeting has concluded. Give yourself the opportunity to allow that to happen virtually as well.

After a one-on-one meeting ends, just switch back to rapport.

> "Well, the next steps seem to be A, B, and C. Yes? [Buyer agrees.]

> Great. Before you go, while we have a few minutes, curious to know more about what you said about being a part-time professional chef. Sounds interesting."

You can also make a similar statement instead of asking a question as it still invites a response.

> "Well, the next steps seem to be A, B, and C. Yes? [Buyer agrees.]

> Great. Ah, now it's Friday. Kids are away. Husband is away. I'm going to play thirty-six holes of golf and drink fruity drinks with umbrellas. You?" «Pause for reaction and laugh, similar weekend comment, chat ensues.»

If it's a group meeting, one-on-one rapport is a little more difficult to do. But it's easy enough. It works great to say, "Angie, everyone is hopping off, but do you have another minute to chat?" If Angie says yes, then you can ask your question once everyone is gone and see where it goes.

To do this, you might say something like,

"Angie, while we've been working on this project for four months, you and I have never had the chance to speak except about the work we're trying to sort out. I'd like to learn more about you and how you'd like to see all this play out. Can we grab fifteen minutes later this week?"

You might not set every meeting, but if you don't ask, you won't get *any* meetings. Even if you don't get the meeting, most people will be impressed.

Small meetings built for rapport-building (e.g., coffee shop)

Sometimes, for reasons of geography, travel, time, pandemics (hopefully not too much of this one anymore), or whatever, it's difficult, if not impossible, to get together to chat over coffee, meals, or at local events. But sellers should feel free to reach out just to make the connection, catch up, or talk, especially with people you know, and for professionals and sellers who tend to work and network locally.

It's especially important to take the lead and reach out to folks to set up brief meetings to connect, especially in times of economic, health, or global crises. These are the conditions under which people seek connection. You'll get more yesses on requests for shorter fifteen- or twenty-minute meetings than longer ones, and often meetings run longer anyway.

For example, in an email you might write:

Hi Carl, it's been a while and I was thinking of you because «insert reason here». Given «insert reason here», I thought it might be good to catch up on a call. Up for it? – Susan

Yes, it can be that simple. You don't have to mention video either. If they say yes, just send the meeting notice with video credentials using the language in Chapter 3 to mention that you'll be logging into video.

Large meetings (e.g., industry events)

It's hard to replace large meetings. When you can, it's definitely a good idea to make the effort to attend. But when circumstances preclude in-person attendance, you can take the lead to bring people together virtually.

For example, you could set up video calls for peers to talk. Let's say you're an accountant. You want to have discussions with CFOs.

Ask one of your clients if they'd be interested in joining a peer call one night. When they say yes, then reach out to other clients that you want to maintain and grow, and potentially to new clients, with a message like this. (Of course, ask permission to use their name when inviting others.)

> «NAME»,
>
> We haven't met, but I'm reaching out because you're the CFO at «COMPANY». And based on your LinkedIn profile, we know twenty-one of the same people including «Person, person, and person».
>
> I'm organizing a call with six CFOs in the next few weeks to talk about «agenda items 1, 2, and 3» and generally to get to know each other. Jane Smith, at CFO at BigCo will be there. Would you like to join?
>
> Any questions?
>
> Regards,
>
> «NAME»

It's customized, it's value-adding, it's connection-developing. It's good selling all around.

Rapport-building around, but not at, meetings

Beyond meetings, there are other ways to build rapport and make connections that virtual sellers use well, especially striking up conversations by email, LinkedIn, text, or other messaging media. Don't neglect to make the most of these opportunities. Too many emails, for example, are written without evidence of an individual's personal flair so they often sound bland and impersonal. Take a chance and put some personality in yours.

Chapter 4 Key Takeaways

- **Buyers buy more often** from people they feel connected to and with whom they have trusted relationships. Sellers need to build rapport that formerly was easier to manage in **face-to**-face settings.

- **Sellers who take the lead** proactively create opportunity, time, and space for **rapport-building** virtually.

- **To build rapport,** be planful about engaging, before, during, and after virtual meetings and even via email or social web. Attend to these four principles:
  1. Empathy: Be curious. Listen. Care.
  2. Authenticity: Be real.
  3. Similarity: Find common ground.
  4. Shared Experience: Interact.

CHAPTER 5

LEADING A VIRTUAL NEEDS DISCOVERY: HOW TO UNCOVER ASPIRATIONS AND AFFLICTIONS

ASPIRATIONS AND AFFLICTIONS—THE LETTERS REPRESENTING NEEDS DISCOVERY—ARE THE *A* IN RAIN SELLING.

To learn more about RAIN Selling, visit the *Virtual Selling* book tools on the RAIN Group website for free content (http://raingrp. com/VS-BookTools), or pick up a copy of the *Wall Street Journal* bestselling book, *Rainmaking Conversations*.

How to Discover Needs—A Brief Summary

Most sales advice suggests that to sell products and services as solutions to needs, you must first uncover the problems and pains of your buyers (their afflictions). Uncovering your buyer's afflictions is a crucial step in the sales process.

The reasons are simple:

- If the buyer communicates her business afflictions to you, then it is likely that she wants them to go away if possible. And she is also inevitably considering whether it makes sense to invest the time, money, and brainpower to eliminate them.
- Each affliction you uncover gives you the chance to explore it fully to discover its true and full impact, both rational and emotional.

- Uncovering and discussing one affliction can lead to other afflictions, which the buyer may not have been thinking about in the first place.

But afflictions only focus on half—the negative half—of the buyer's needs. If you focus only on the negative, you miss much of your chance to uncover visions, goals, hopes, and untapped opportunities.

When buyers buy, they could be thinking, or at least be led to think, as much about aspirations (the future they are seeking) as they are about afflictions (the problems they'd like to fix).

If you ask questions exclusively in the negative, you'll tend to probe for needs that way. You'll ask questions like: "Where are you unhappy with performance?" "What keeps you up at night?" "Where is the pain?"

But, if you consider a buyer's aspirations as much as their afflictions, you'll remember to ask future-seeking as well as problem-solving questions—questions with themes such as: "Where do you want to take the business?" "What are the possibilities?"

Needs discovery is not only about asking questions. A buyer might say at this point, "What are the possibilities? I wish I knew!" If they do, it gives you the opportunity to share possibilities and stoke their desire.

In our *Top Virtual Selling Challenges and Priorities* research, buyers told us just how important this is to them: 68 percent said that when sellers show them what's possible or how to solve a problem it has a high level of influence on their purchase decision. Unfortunately, only 34 percent said sellers do this well in their virtual interactions.

If you ask questions and share possibilities that look to the future, you will find that—instead of just bringing some aspirin for the pain—you will help paint the most compelling, impactful, and comprehensive vision of a new and better reality for your buyers.

Differences in Needs Discovery— Face-to-Face vs. Virtual Selling

Consider how Aspirations and Afflictions rank on the Virtual Selling Divergence Scale, a measure of how different a component of selling is when comparing face-to-face vs. virtual selling.

1. Not that much different
2. A little different
3. Somewhat different
4. Different
5. Significantly different

Uncovering Aspirations and Afflictions during Needs Discovery—a key component of Case-Making, is a **4 out of 5 different**. It's different. Here's how.

Component	Face-to-Face	Virtual Selling
Preparation and pre-meeting	• Best to use a RAIN Sales Conversation Planner to prepare needs questions but many salespeople wing it	• Also best to use a RAIN Sales Conversation Planner, but, importantly, *there's less buyer tolerance for winging it in virtual meetings,* meandering, dead air, and off-point questions will lose buyer attention and upend the meeting
	• Many sellers don't ask questions via email or survey before meetings	• Opportunity to share questions in advance and get answers; buyers more open to needs discovery surveys

Component	Face-to-Face	Virtual Selling
Leading the meeting	• Can take notes in notebooks, but typing can be a distraction depending on the meeting and buyer dynamics • Difficult to have planned questions in front of you as it looks like a rookie who needs a cheat sheet	• Much easier to take notes by typing, but best to keep eyes in the right spot (the camera) or risk disengagement; can take needs discovery notes with buyer watching; buyers often find this engaging • Can easily have needs discovery notes in front of you, and easier to have cheat sheets on second screens or paper not visible to buyer
After meetings	Asking preparatory and follow-up questions by email is a good idea, but some buyers prefer to do everything live, not having more involved email discussions	Buyers more tolerant and open to email when all is virtual; opportunity for sellers to be more organized, thorough, and impressive

Uncovering Aspirations and Afflictions— Needs Discovery in a Virtual Selling World

It wasn't long ago that selling was almost 100 percent face-to-face or on the telephone. Crazy as it might seem, it's really only in the last ten years or so that true digital natives—people who are often more comfortable typing than talking—have found themselves in decision-making positions.

Until 2020, the switch to virtual selling was gradual. For many sellers, even though many meetings would take place via screen share, and communications were largely via email in between meetings, the meat of the selling happened during live discussions.

Now it's mostly blended, but sometimes 100 percent virtual.

This change hasn't altered the fundamentals of needs discovery. Yes, in some ways needs discovery is more difficult, but this shift gives organized sellers a greater advantage.

As 71 percent of buyers told us in our research, the seller's ability to lead a thorough discovery of concerns, wants, and needs in their virtual interactions has a high level of influence on buyer purchase decisions. But only 26 percent of buyers agree sellers are very effective here, with 74 percent either neutral or negative on seller effectiveness.

The shift to virtual makes unorganized sellers' faults more pronounced, and differentiates those who are more prepared, skilled, and thorough.

Preparation

Too many sellers think the shift to virtual simply means adding video to meetings. It's so much more; virtual selling significantly alters the dynamics of how buyers want, and are willing, to interact with sellers.

One buyer told us recently,

> "One of the things I can't stand is when I get on a meeting with a seller, after they've had their initial qualification meeting (which I had to tolerate), they ask me a bunch of questions that I could have answered more accurately, more thoroughly, and more quickly via email or a standard survey. And if I had the questions in advance, I could have passed them off to a specialist on my team who could answer them for me more accurately, and the process would move faster."

If you know you need answers to background questions, and you know you need answers to preference, wants, and needs questions, consider sending them in advance. Here's what happens when you do.

- You might get all the answers, and more answers than you could gather in a call. Then when you have the call you use the live web meeting time more fruitfully.
- If this happens, the sales cycle is shorter because you reduce the need to have more follow-up meetings. You get your answers *before the meetings.*
- Buyers will answer, via survey or email, and if it's their preference, sometimes you will engage in discussion via email, speeding up the process even more.
- Buyers say, "I don't have time to answer these questions right now, but thanks for sending them along. Let's cover them in the meeting." You might never know it, but buyers often read them and think about them, and you gain their attention.

In other words, you can move the process along more quickly, get more and better information, and impress buyers.

Also, to the extent you can customize your questions for that specific buyer, you build more trust and can help buyers see that you are a cut above the rest.

Here's an example email you might send, which of course you could always send via survey as well.

Steve,

Looking forward to our meeting on the 17th. I know you are keen to figure out what to do here. To help the process along, see below for background questions that we'll need to answer as we figure out the right solution for you and when the time is right to craft a proposal. If you or someone on your team can take a crack at it this would be great.

1. In the last six months I've spoken to a number of people who said that competitor X is about twice as fast in «area» as you are. What's your take on needing to speed up to catch them, and how do you think you might go about that?

2. In our experience, three factors make a difference in driving operational efficiencies that make a huge difference in X. They are A, B, and C. Do you think you need work in these areas? If so, what and how?

3. Folks have told me that you have tried to make strides in «area» in the past, but the efforts stalled. Why would you say they stalled?

4. Let's say it actually works out that, in three months, you successfully accomplish «goal». How do you think that would affect the business?

5. If there were three issues that were top of mind in «this area» to tackle, what are they and why?

Of course, there's more we can cover, but to the degree that we can get through this list I think we'll have a sense of whether we can help, what the best way forward would be, and how to make sure it gets the outcomes you're looking for.

To the extent you'd like, please answer by email. Of course, we can always pick it up at the meeting if you'd prefer, but this will give you a sense of what I'm thinking would be good to cover.

Did I hit the mark? Anything you'd suggest for changes?

Looking forward to your thoughts and the call.

«Signature»

Whether you use pre-live needs discovery email questions or not, you'll want to prepare for virtual meetings in a standard way. Here's an example of the RAIN Group Sales Conversation Planner, that you can download from the *Virtual Selling* book tools section of the RAIN Group website (http://raingrp.com/VS-BookTools).

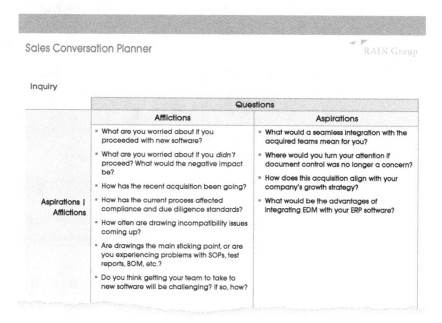

FIGURE 5.1 Aspirations and Afflictions

Leading the Meeting

After pleasantries, it's time for needs discovery. In an in-person meeting, it may not be good form to pull out your Sales Conversation Planner, but in a virtual meeting, you can have it right in front of you on paper if you like, or on the screen.

To probe the buyer's needs, you must prepare your questions in advance. A common question that sellers have for us is how to make sure, when they share their screens, that buyers don't see the prepared list of questions. It depends on your platform, but most screen-sharing technologies allow selective screen sharing. However, you might try sharing the questions with the buyer on the screen deliberately.

A participant in one of our training programs said to us,

"I had it up and it was great! This has been helping a lot. But then I shared my screen, and a buyer saw my questions. I thought for a minute that I made a mistake, and was embarrassed, but something happened that really surprised me. The buyer said, 'This is impressive. I wish every salesperson prepared for our meetings as thoroughly as it seems you have. Let's go through your questions and see where we get to.'"

Commonly, sellers don't think they should share prepared questions, but why not? Buyers tend to like it.

Another advantage of virtual meetings is that screen share is, for the most part, expected. A rarely used, but often very powerful needs discovery tool, is to share one visual that will prompt buyers to share their needs, without you even having to ask any questions.

Recall the RAIN Group Sales Competency Wheel™ in Chapter 1. When we're speaking with our prospective clients, we'll often put that up on the screen as a prompt for figuring out what skills would be most important for a sales team at a particular company to develop.

FIGURE 5.2 Screen Share an Online Prompt to Encourage Buyers to Share Needs

We share it and say something like this,

> "Have a look at the Sales Competency Wheel. These are common areas where sellers need to be skilled to succeed.
>
> How do you think you're doing in the various areas? Anything jump out that, if your team made great improvements, would move the needle a lot?"

Then the buyers share, typically quite openly and thoroughly.

If buyers leave out areas that are often important, we ask clarifying questions. For example, to dig into opportunity management, we at RAIN Group might ask question such as: Do you feel like sellers are doing everything they should to win important sales? Do you feel your selling process maps accurately to the way your buyers like to buy? What are some disconnects?

We could add dozens more but the point is these are pretty in-depth questions that would be difficult to have in front of you as a seller in a face-to-face meeting, but in a virtual meeting, with the ease that we've discussed, sellers can easily have the cheat sheets right in front of them.

RAIN Group—Major Capabilities, Needs, and Messages

Capability Area	Needs/ Triggers	Impact		General Talking Points	Questions to Uncover Need
		Talking Points	Calculate		

FIGURE 5.3   RAIN Group Needs Discovery Guide, Template

Again, there's an advantage in virtual selling in the area of needs discovery for sellers who are prepared. Those sellers who take the lead in being more organized than the sellers who just aren't trying as hard, gain a competitive edge with buyers.

After Meetings

After the meeting, virtual selling has additional advantages vs. face-to-face selling.

- Sellers can send the buyer a recording of the meeting.
- You can edit the recording so the hour of discussion boils down to twenty or so important minutes. (Many sellers are surprised at how often buyers will share tight, edited recordings among their peers).
- You can post the recording in a virtual sales document repository that enables you to view who has accessed files.
- Sellers can easily summarize in email, a document or, even more impressive, via a three-minute video what you heard and what you think you can do. Ask if you are on target or missed anything important.

Of course, you won't use these for every buyer, but to the extent that an opportunity is important, these buyer-focused strategies are available to sellers willing to take the lead and use them.

Chapter 5 Key Takeaways

- **Seventy-one percent of buyers** told us in our research that a seller's ability to lead a thorough discovery of concerns, wants, and needs in their virtual interactions has a high level of influence on purchase decisions.

- **Buyers also tell us** that sellers often fall short, and too few execute virtual needs discovery well.

- **The most successful sellers:**
  - Explore the full set of buyer needs by uncovering both Aspirations and Afflictions.
  - Are more organized, thorough, and impressive in the discovery process.
  - Use planning tools and pre-written questions, and show them live in virtual discovery sessions.
  - Gather more and better information, often speeding up the sales process, by sending background questions in advance.
  - Customize questions for each buyer.
    (http://raingrp.com/VS-BookTools).

CHAPTER 6

MAKING THE IMPACT
AND ROI CASE

IMPACT IS THE *I* IN RAIN SELLING.

To learn more about RAIN Selling, visit the *Virtual Selling* book tools on the RAIN Group website for free content (http://raingrp.com/VS-BookTools), or pick up a copy of the *Wall Street Journal* bestselling book, *Rainmaking Conversations*.

Thinking about Impact

Consider a change that many people want to achieve at some point in their lives: eating better and exercising more.

You might think that changing your exercise and nutrition regimen or adopting a new one is something a person does unaided. That might be true for some people, but according to market-research.com, the total U.S. weight loss market in 2019 was $72.7 billion. This represents the spending on people and products that help other people eat and exercise better.

But you can't measure the ROI of weight loss (typically) in monetary terms because the ROI is essentially emotional.

The point is this: emotions are powerful motivators of buying. People buy with their hearts and justify with their minds. Even in business, decisions are *driven* by wants, desires, and fears. They are then *justified* by rational return on investment cases.

Buyers need the ROI case to justify their purchase decisions, but, for the most part, they're not getting it from sellers. While 66 percent of business-to-business buyers who buy virtually say that when sellers make the ROI case clear it has a high influence on their likelihood to purchase, they find only 16 percent of sellers very effective at it.[1]

In fact, of fifteen different seller skills we studied through the eyes of the buyers, sellers were worst—fifteenth out of fifteen—in "making the return on investment (ROI) case clear to me."

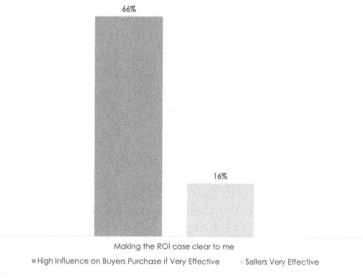

FIGURE 6.1 Making the ROI Case Clear to Buyers

When it comes to impact and ROI case-making, there are many general misconceptions sellers have that lead to lower sales results. Consider the following information we've learned from our work with over 1,000 sales organizations and through decades of analysis at the RAIN Group Center for Sales Research.

What sellers think	What's more often true
Impact is about the financial case, the hard ROI numbers	ROI cases are used by buyers to rationalize their decisions and sell them internally to peers, but the decisions are largely emotional
I know how to make the ROI case; I'm good at this	Only 16 percent of *buyers* believe sellers are very effective making their ROI case[2] Interestingly, sellers are twice as likely as buyers are to think that they can make the ROI case well[3]
I'll show them the ROI case and it'll be impressive	Buyer's think, "Another load-of-bull ROI calculator from a seller who probably doesn't even understand the numbers anyway. I could tear this case to shreds."
I'll show them the ROI and that'll be enough	You have to show buyers the ROI in the context of a new reality or it may even *hurt your chances of success* (more on this below); and you have to get buyers to believe deeply the ROI is reasonably achievable

When it comes to impact, here's what's most important to know:

- Making the ROI case is critical to success; don't make a case, and you are more likely to lose.
- It's of critical importance that you make the ROI case *plausible* and *believable*. Even if sellers can make the ROI case, they underestimate the effort needed to get buyers to accept and support the ROI case itself. Buyers chuckle under their breath at how often sellers use ROI calculators.
- How you *build and present* the ROI case is, we'd argue, even more important than the details of the case itself. In fact, you can use virtual selling to your advantage here.

Presenting ROI the Wrong Way Correlates with a 27 Percent Drop in Win Rates

Consider an analysis of tens of thousands of sales calls by revenue intelligence platform Gong. Ineffective attempts by sellers to present ROI correlate with deals going south.

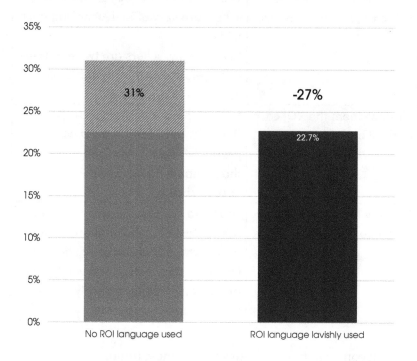

FIGURE 6.2   Effect of Presenting Implausible or Unbelievable ROI

Gong's findings support our point that you need to *make* your ROI case, and not just talk about or present it. They even note it's possible "presenting ROI *does* work, but most salespeople do it so naively that it backfires" and that "most attempts at presenting ROI are a desperate Hail Mary to save hopeless deals."

Probably both are true often enough. We'd add that in our experience, many sellers throw around ROI numbers willy-nilly that they say are "often achieved" with their solution, but they don't make the ROI case for the specific buyer; they don't even attempt it.

Gong goes on to say the best advice is to tell a before-and-after customer story. We agree and cover this approach (new reality) in the next chapter. But first, let's address how to build the ROI case effectively before presenting it the right way.

Differences in Impact— Face-to-Face vs. Virtual Selling

Consider how impact ranks on the Virtual Selling Divergence Scale, a measure of how different a component of selling is when comparing face-to-face vs. virtual selling:

1. Not that much different
2. A little different
3. Somewhat different
4. Different
5. Significantly different

Impact, a key component of case-making, is a **4 out of 5 different**. It's different. Here's how.

Component	Face-to-Face	Virtual Selling
Rational: Gathering the data needed to calculate ROI	Often done live in meetings; seller takes notes on notepad or white board	• Sellers find it difficult to gather data on screen share or video calls • Data can be gathered at meetings, but the nature of virtual selling opens the door for data collection via email

Component	Face-to-Face	Virtual Selling
Rational: Building the ROI case	Rarely done interactively; mostly built by seller and presented at future meeting	Easier access to computers and screen sharing make it even easier to collaborate to build the case, but few sellers know how to do this
Rational: General (not financial) impact points (a.k.a. benefits)	Sellers not consistent or thorough about gathering the impact data that are a few steps away from benefits and can be translated directly to financials (e.g., more motivated team, more positive culture, more innovation)*	Medium provides advantages to sellers to be systematic about general impact points, but sellers rarely take advantage of it
Emotional	Typically neglected by sellers, but the intimacy of face-to-face interaction puts buyers more at ease; more likely they will state desires and fears	Typically neglected by sellers, and doesn't happen organically as often as it does in face-to-face selling; sellers must create conditions to allow emotional impact to come to the fore

---

* It's an advanced sales, business, and financial literacy skill, but anything like this can be plausible and defensibly stated in financial terms.

Component	Face-to-Face	Virtual Selling
Rational and emotional: Presenting a unified, persuasive impact case	• Typically presented as ROI verbally, as bullets in a proposal, or weakly in a spreadsheet graphic; rarely as impactful as it should be • Typically, not presented as an integrated rational and emotional story	• Opportunity for sellers to leverage all the elements of a virtual meeting to present a rational and emotional impact in one integrated narrative story • Good initial data collection enables time to craft a narrative

Impact and ROI in a Virtual Selling World

Know Your Impact Model

The first step in demonstrating ROI is gathering the data you need for your impact model. Your impact model is the mix of assumptions that, should they be affected, result in a financial change. Regardless of the type of selling, many sellers don't know what data they need so they don't gather it at all. Instead, they rely on weak and lazy arguments that go something like, "on average, our clients achieve a 7 percent revenue lift when they buy and implement our software."

This isn't good enough for most buyers. They need to see what *their* ROI might be.

In the next step, we'll cover what to do with this data. But first you need to gather the data: Know what data you need and ask for it.

In face-to-face selling, we've observed most sellers ask for the data they need in a meeting, then record it, and—if they're good— use it for analysis and presentation later. Sometimes a seller may model out their impact directly at a white board, but this is rare. The point is this: Data is usually gathered live.

Virtual selling opens the door to email and survey-focused data gathering.

Let's assume you know what data you need to demonstrate your ROI. You can ask for it in a first or subsequent meeting, after a meeting via email, or after a meeting via survey. You might say,

> "One of the things I'd like to do is make some assumptions that can show the impact of doing «XYZ». Would you kindly answer the following five questions? If you're comfortable, please respond via email. If not, let's discuss at our next talk on Thursday. Meanwhile, if you send the responses by Wednesday a.m. I'll be able to develop some scenarios we can play with together to see what the ROI case might be."

If you're talking to a C-level or senior buyer, you might ask them, "Is there someone I can talk to so I can gather some technical data to model out how doing «XYZ» will have an impact in the areas we talked about?" This is an underused, yet very effective technique. Sometimes senior buyers don't have the time to personally respond to your inquiry, but they are happy to make sure you get information from someone else. And once a senior buyer asks someone else at their company to do something, it often gets done.

In any case, whether via call, email, or survey all of this happens virtually.

Build the ROI Case Collaboratively

In Chapter 10, How to Collaborate with Buyers Virtually, we cover the power of collaboration. In a nutshell: when you do something—like build an ROI case—for a buyer it's yours, psychologically speaking. They don't own it and they're not invested in it. When you do it together, however, that changes. To the extent someone does something themselves, and to the degree it was challenging and engaging, it becomes important to them. They're invested in it.

That is why we encourage you to build the ROI case collaboratively with your buyer.

In Chapter 1, Great Selling, Done Virtually, we demonstrated the ROI that could be achieved through virtual selling. For illustration purposes, here it is again.

Impact Model: Face-to-Face vs. Virtual					
Note: Numbers rounded for illustration purposes					
Current State: Face-to-Face			Future State: Virtual		
Pipeline Metrics		Conversion Rate	Pipeline Metrics		Conversion Rate
Meetings	230		Meetings	345	
Pipeline	115	50%	Pipeline	173	50%
Proposals	46	40%	Proposals	70	40%
Wins	20	42%	Wins	30	42%
Avg size	$100,000		Avg size	$100,000	
Total sales per seller	$2,000,000		Total sales per seller	$3,000,000	
# of sellers	100		# of sellers	100	
Sales per year	$200,000,000		Sales per year	$300,000,000	
			Increase	$100,000,000	
Avg sales mtgs per day	1		Avg sales mtgs per day	1.5	
Selling days per year	230		Selling days per year	230	
Meetings per year	230		Meetings per year	345	
% days travel	50%		% days travel	10%	
Travel days per year	115		Travel days per year	23	
Travel costs per day	$1,200		Travel costs per day	$1,200	
Travel costs per seller per year	$138,000		Travel costs per seller per year	$27,600	
Travel costs per yr total	$13,800,000		Travel costs per yr total	$2,760,000	
			Cost Savings	$11,040,000	
			Total Impact	$111,040,000	
56% revenue growth by transitioning to virtual selling					

FIGURE 6.3 Building the ROI Case Collaboratively, Example #1

Constructing the impact model here is pretty simple:

- Four pipeline metrics
- Number of sellers
- Average size of sale
- Average days of travel per year per seller
- Average travel cost per day

That's all it takes to create a chart based on metrics most sales organizations have on hand or can closely estimate. Change some assumptions and voilà! Huge differences.

Here's are two real-life scenarios when these numbers—even the same numbers—are arrived at in two different ways.

Analysis process	Outcome
We ask for metrics, make some reasonable assumptions, and present them to buyers.	Disengagement. Challenges. Sometimes discussion that leads to collaborative changing of assumptions.
We ask for metrics then *ask collaborative questions* where buyers make some assumption changes themselves.	Engagement, interest, excitement, collaborative iteration.

The second scenario certainly achieves better outcomes than the first.

Now, here's an example of what happens in a virtual selling situation—a different example, but the same assumption set.

RAIN Group Consultant: Thanks for sending along the core sales metrics for the average folks on the team and for the top performers. What I'd like to do is take five minutes to try to figure out what might be plausible to get the averages up.

Corporate Sales Leader: Okay, let's do it.

RAIN Group Consultant: You mentioned that your sellers on average have 200 first conversations per year. Fifty percent of those hit the pipeline, 40 percent of those go to proposal, and you have a 42 percent win rate. And they have an average sale size of $100k.

Your top performers have 240 new opportunities because they prospect more, turn 60 percent into pipeline opportunities because they are more impressive in initial discussions, move 48 percent to proposal, and win 55 percent of proposals. And they have an average sale size of $132k because of better cross-selling and solution crafting?

Metric	Average Performers	Top Performers
Leads	200	240
Pipeline Opportunities	100 (50%)	144 (60%)
Proposals	40 (40%)	70 (48%)
Wins	17 (42%)	39 (55%)
Average size of sale	$100,000	$132,000

FIGURE 6.4 Sample Metrics Average vs. Top Performers

Corporate Sales Leader: Yes, indeed.

RAIN Group Consultant: Okay, talk to me for a minute about what a new average could be. What could we plausibly push leads to?

Corporate Sales Leader: Well, I think even top performers have a way to go higher, but let's be realistic. There's no reason they can't get to 10 percent more, so I guess 220 on average.

RAIN Group Consultant: And pipeline opportunities?

Corporate Sales Leader: I've listened to many calls. They're okay, but some of them are awful and most of them could be so much better! It's no wonder only 50 percent move along on average after first calls—percent for sure.

RAIN Group Consultant: You mentioned your CFO is really conservative and skeptical though. Should we take any of these metrics and mimic top performers?

Corporate Sales Leader: Good point. Let's make it 55 percent

RAIN Group Consultant: Reasonable? Proposals and wins?

Corporate Sales Leader: Okay, to be completely defensible to my own team, I'd say 45 percent to proposal and 47 percent win rate are realistically achievable. And average size of sale: $120k.

RAIN Group Consultant: We've seen that be even more challenging to achieve than moving win rates up. Let's only raise it 5 percent.

Corporate Sales Leader: Well, I'm positive, with some effort we could achieve that. Question is, will it be worth the effort?

RAIN Group Consultant: Let's take a look. I didn't make the final assumptions, I left them blank so you could make them, but here we go. And let's not even increase the leads. If the pipelines are that much fuller, let's not fight sellers to push leads even more.

Corporate Sales Leader: Well, I could sell that to them. Let's see what my numbers come out to.

RAIN Group Consultant: One moment... Here we go.

Impact Calculator

Sales Results -- Goals and Assumptions							
Current State				**Future State**			
		Conversion Rate				Conversion Rate	
Leads	200			Leads	200		
Pipeline	100	50%		Pipeline	110	55%	
Proposals	40	40%		Proposals	50	45%	
Wins	17	42%		Wins	24	47%	
Avg size	$100,000			Avg size	$105,000		
Sales per Seller	$1,700,000				$2,520,000		
# of Sellers	100				100		
Sales per Year	$170,000,000				$252,000,000		
				Increase	$82,000,000		

FIGURE 6.5 Building the ROI Case Collaboratively, Example #2

Corporate Sales Leader: Wait a minute. We barely moved some of the metrics and you kept pulling me back to be "more reasonable," and yet we could grow the company by 86 percent if we just changed these metrics a little.

RAIN Group Sales Leader: Yes, you don't even need to approximate the results of the best people on the team. You just need to move several metrics in the right direction.

Corporate Sales Leader: Impressive. The case works. Now, how do we get there? You still have to convince me we can achieve these numbers.

RAIN Group Sales Leader: Well, let's talk about it. How well do you think the team is doing right now with...

You get the idea. The point is, with virtual selling, you can get data you need beforehand, then, because you're typically on a computer in virtual selling; it's natural to do this collaboratively.

Rational: General (Not Financial) Impact Points

As we noted earlier, almost any assumption that you change about a business can be translated into actual financial impact. But sometimes the leap is not as linear as in the example above with changes to sales pipeline metrics.

Here's where virtual selling has advantages over face-to-face: screens. When it's time to have the discussion about impact, whether it's a sophisticated tool or a simple list, open your impact list and ask questions or make points about various areas that might resonate with your buyer.

Common business factors that affect financial impact, some with linear financial cases and some not, include:

- Reduced cycle times
- Increased uptime
- Lower risk
- Faster time to market
- Increased sales person performance
- Strengthened innovation
- Higher profitability
- Higher employee engagement
- Less waste
- Increased leads in the pipeline
- Lower cost in any area while maintaining or improving quality
- Better quality/fewer repairs/longer life
- Increased brand recognition or preference
- Less employee turnover
- Fewer stops and starts of projects
- Less scrap and rework
- Higher employee productivity

Let's take one example from the list above: higher employee engagement. If this was a possible impact point for your buyers, but you weren't sure, you could have it on your screen as a part of your needs discovery graphic.

You ask a question about it, the buyer says she does think it's a concern, and you have a conversation. You offer to do a complementary confidential survey of, say, thirty people on her team to measure their level of engagement. It turns out, they are just below average: forty-fifth percentile.

Then you can lead a collaborative discussion about the various things you can do to change that. Let's say you get to the point where the buyer believes engagement can go way up, you can share validated industry data that reads like:

> The most "engaged" workplaces (those in the top 25 percent) were 50 percent more likely to have lower turnover, 56 percent more likely to have higher-than-average customer loyalty, 38 percent more likely to have above-average productivity, and 27 percent more likely to report higher profitability.[4]

Even something as "soft" as employee engagement can, with just a few leaps, work its way over to a figure you can calculate into ROI. There's a calculable cost to replace any employee that turns over (recruiting costs, lost productivity), calculable impact to each employee's productivity (e.g., shifting from X output per employee to Y), and profitability itself is a calculation.

No matter what, you can make an impact case. Taking the lead with virtual tools—screens, surveys, calculators, and so on—can not only make a seller's life easier it can make them more successful.

Making the Emotional Case

Making the rational case is, of its nature, pretty cut and dried: You know how to do the math, you gather the data to do the math, you talk about what math need to change, and you calculate impact.

The emotional case can be a little more challenging in a virtual sale, mainly because of the more intimate feel of live meetings And in the case of live multi-person meetings, it's easier to break away to talk one-on-one for a bit.

We won't get into detail about how to uncover emotional needs. For more on that, pick up a copy of the book *Rainmaking Conversations*.[5] But imagine for a moment, at its simplest, the following:

- You're in a face-to-face sales meeting and have a fruitful sales conversation with three stakeholders that ends at 2 p.m. The key decision-maker walks you out. On the way out, you say, "During the part of the conversation when we talked about «topic», you seemed, I don't know, worried? Skeptical? How are you feeling about it all?"
- The buyer says, "Well we tried this in the past and it failed very publicly, with the egg on my face. I'm wondering why this time it'll be different. The more junior players on the team are fired up to do this, but they haven't been humiliated publicly like I was ten years ago at another company."
- You say, "Okay, do you have ten minutes to show me where I can get some coffee, and we can talk along the way?"
- Decision-maker, "Sure. Let's go."
- Same situation, but this time it's a virtual meeting with this group. It ends at 2 p.m. then it's over. You saw the pained look on the buyer's face during the meeting. At 2 p.m. everyone hangs up! No walk to coffee. No organic conversation possible.

In this case, you need to take the lead. Call or email the person right away and say, "I'd like two more minutes for one question. Can we talk?" *Create the conditions to make the conversation happen.* Take the lead and you can get to the same result, but under no circumstances should you just sit back and hope for the best.

Rational and Emotional: Presenting a Unified, Persuasive Impact Case

This chapter is about how to build your impact case virtually. In the next, we cover how to present the impact case, in context, so that it is as persuasive and compelling as possible.

Chapter 6 Key Takeaways

- **Only 16 percent of buyers** believe that virtual sellers are very effective at making ROI cases. Therefore, success follows sellers who understand how to make the case virtually.

- **Expert case-making engages buyers' emotions,** as well as their rational minds and virtual selling provides ample opportunities to make a rational, **ROI-focused** impact case that is plausible and believable. Know:
  - Virtual tools, such as screens, surveys, and ROI calculators, can help you make a powerful emotional and rational impact case.
  - How you build and present the ROI case is even more important than the details of the case itself.
  - Know what data you need to demonstrate your ROI case and ask for it ahead of time.
  - Collaborate with buyers to create the impact model. Doing so engages their interest and excitement, increases their sense of investment and ownership, and moves them emotionally and rationally.

MAKING THE CASE FOR CHANGE: PAINTING THE PICTURE OF THE NEW REALITY

NEW REALITY IS THE _N_ IN RAIN SELLING.

To learn more about RAIN Selling, visit the _Virtual Selling_ book tools on the RAIN Group website for free content (http://raingrp. com/VS-BookTools), or pick up a copy of the _Wall Street Journal_ bestselling book, _Rainmaking Conversations_.

**Authors' note:** _This chapter sets up the construct for making the overall case for change, which is vital to your success as a seller. The content is equally relevant to face-to-face selling and virtual selling._

How to build and deliver that case virtually follows in the subsequent two chapters, Chapter 8, Inspiring Buyers with New Ideas Virtually, and Chapter 9, Delivering Powerful Virtual Proposal Presentations.

New Reality—The Case for Change on a Page

It's not a bold statement to say that the job of a leader is to drive change. But when we at RAIN Group suggest to our clients that driving change is the primary objective of a seller's job, even if they're selling something as straightforward as office supplies, we get more than a few sideways glances.

We stand by this assertion: A seller's job is to drive change.

As we introduced back in Chapter 2, sellers do this by making the case to buyers for their new reality around priorities, approaches, impact, decisions, and partners. The mantra is: *"Do this, not that… this way, not that… because. Act now, not later… with us, not them."*

Making the new reality case brings everything together because it contains all the key elements of the case for change on one page.

Now, do all sellers always need to make every case here? No. However, it's prudent to make the whole case rock solid for each sale.

Category	When needed	Not needed when	Yet sometimes...
Priorities: "Do this, not that"	You need to put a new priority at the top of a buyer's to-do list	Buyer has already decided to do something	Approaching decision time, another priority arises and trumps yours; or another buyer joins the decision team late and doesn't see the benefit
Approaches: "This way, not that"	When the buyer needs to change how they approach something	When the buyer has already decided to change their approach to yours	A buyer considers yet another approach that you don't know about

Category	When needed	Not needed when	Yet sometimes...
Impact: "Because"	Almost always	When the buyer *must* do something and has *zero alternatives* (i.e., you're the only plumber there and a pipe burst), or for whatever reason they would never choose someone else	There's no "yet sometimes" here: if you don't have a good "because" answer for almost all of your sales, you won't win much
Decisions: "Act now, not later"	When there's any chance at all they could make no decision at all, or delay for any length of time	When the buyer is urgently dead set on doing something right now	You think it's urgent, they say it's urgent, it's all in the bag; then there's a delay of three days and a new competitor comes in, your buyer loses their job, the buyer's company gets sold, they lose their budgets, coronavirus, locusts—these happen all the time

Category	When needed	Not needed when	Yet sometimes...
Partners: "With us, not them"	When the buyer has any alternative: other vendors, internal staff, or any other option	Sole source with no internal options	There's another hidden competitor, a late entrant, an internal power play, or some buyer doesn't feel confident in you, so they scuttle the whole thing

In our experience, a transformation occurs not when we *tell* clients a seller's job is change, but when we *involve them in the discussion* and they conclude it for themselves. In other words, we make the case collaboratively.

Here's an example of various questions we, at RAIN Group, might ask our clients relating to their sales challenges, and examples of the very common answers they give us.

Example question: If buyers aren't spending money on you, are they spending money on anything similar?

Example answer: We're a marketing firm that generates leads. It's insane that so many companies we can help are spending so much of their money on PR firms so they can see their name in lights, but it generates *zero leads*. For the same money, we can fill their pipeline like crazy.

For sellers to succeed here, they need to make a case to change **priorities: Do this... not that!**

Example question: Can you share with me an example of why a buyer might say it's essential to buy from you?

Example answer: Our clients succeed at implementing their CRM technology at a rate of only about 30 percent before buying from us. With us, the success rate is 85 percent. Typically, when they have tried to implement before we come in, they were unaware of many pieces of the puzzle, so the project failed. It shows that some clients have the right priority around implementing CRM, but they *go about it all wrong!*

For sellers to succeed here, they need to make the case to change **approaches: This way, not that!**

Example question: Yes, but on top of a $1 million cost for CRM, adding your implementation services will cost another $300,000? That's a 30 percent increase.

Example answer: First, even if a client would succeed without us which only 30 percent do, we'll help them get it done sixty days faster. That's two months more time to focus on selling vs. CRM. But if they don't succeed, that's $1 million in CRM fees down the tubes, and millions in lost revenue because the sales team and leaders get caught up in a big failed initiative. Let's not forget all the wasted internal staff time. And they're left with nothing if they fail, except a very bad taste in their mouths.

For sellers to succeed here, they need to make the strongest **impact: Because!**

Example question: It looks like about 200 reps on your team have fifty-five-day sales cycles, but about 700 of them have over ninety-day sales cycles, and the sales are the same size. Why?

Example answer: The top 200 reps make the case for urgency. The other 700 don't.

The top 200 reps are better at making the case for buyers to make decisions immediately vs. put off **decisions: Act now, not later.**

Example question: How does performance differ among your best and your average performing sellers?

Example answer: We lose to the competition about 65 percent of the time. Now that's not necessarily bad because we typically compete with three other firms. But our top sellers *beat the competition 65 percent of the time.* Same offerings, same company. Different sellers, wildly different wins and losses vs. competition. The financial difference to us is astronomical.

The top sellers here help buyers see that they need to pick them as **partners: With us, not them!**

Differences in New Reality —Face-to-Face vs. Virtual Selling

Consider how new reality ranks on the Virtual Selling Divergence Scale, a measure of how different a component of selling is when comparing face-to-face vs. virtual selling:

1. Not that much different
2. A little different
3. Somewhat different
4. Different
5. Significantly different

New reality, a key component of case-making, is a **4 out of 5 different**. It's different. Here's how.

Component	Face-to-Face	Virtual Selling
Crafting	In-person conversation with notes and white boards (which are rarely used)	• Live conversations on computer with live shared development • Virtual white boarding with the ability to use a template and populate with buyers in real time
Delivery	Typically, a live conversation or presentation; when really important, an immersive multi-media impressive experience	Presentation via screen share of documents or slides; rarely an immersive or impressive experience

Note the story structures are the same: The new reality summary must fit on a one-page Buyer Change Blueprint. The Convincing

Story framework in the next chapter describes the architecture of how you tell it.

The differences between face-to-face and virtual lie in the crafting and delivery of the new reality.

New Reality in a Virtual Selling World

Eyes on the Prize

If you're a business leader, you might have studied, practiced, and been trained on how to lead and drive change.

If you're a seller, not so much. But there's an easy solution.

When I (Mike) ran my first P&L division at a company, I had the pleasure of working with Dr. Steve Williamson, a visionary in leadership, team development, and change management. Dr. Williamson was the most senior of dozens of industrial/organization (IO) PhDs on staff.

As the leader of the training division, I learned that our clients had a great thirst for learning the basics of organizational development. So, I launched a two-day training program on the topic. It was a huge success and we ended up running it about ten times a year.

I had trouble staffing it, though. As it was a course on the fundamentals, all the IO psychologists on staff said that it was too basic and below them to teach.

All except for Dr. Williamson. He taught it over and over without complaint. I asked him why he was willing all the time to teach this program when our other "experts," though twenty years his junior, weren't. He said simply, "Everything you need to know about organizational development is in the basics course. The more I teach it, the better I am, and I really need to keep reminding myself what it all comes down to. Eyes on the prize, you know."

Change management is like this as well. It all comes down to the basics. We boil it down for you here. There's plenty of nuance to learn, but if you master what's in this chapter, you'll have all you need to succeed.

What Change Is All About

Change is about not being happy in one place, and wanting to be in another place.

Where you are   Where you want to be

FIGURE 7.1 *Change Management*

The intensity of pursuing this change comes down to:

- How much the buyer wants the change.
- How difficult the buyer thinks it will be to get there.
- Their perceived risk of success and failure.

Your job as the seller, then, comes down to:

- Maximizing the buyer's desire and intent to change.
- Making it as painless and simple a process as possible.
- Building buyer belief that it'll work.

That's it. As cliché and simple as it might be, that's what it's all about.

Imagine how successful sellers would be if they could do this.

Buyer Change Blueprint—The Case for Change on a Page

To make the case for change you need to figure out the story driving the change, demonstrate the path to achieve the change and build trust that it'll work.

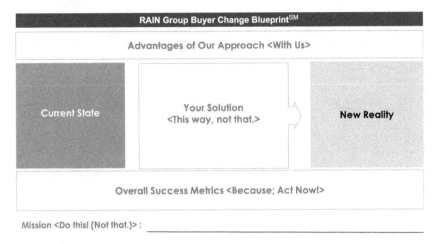

FIGURE 7.2 Buyer Change Blueprint Template

You need to make the solution, the path to getting from Current State to New Reality clear. If you don't illuminate a clear path to change, buyers will be confused about what should happen, what needs to happen, how much work it will take to make it happen, and whether the desired new reality will come true.

You need to make the impact case for doing anything at all (*because*) and doing something with urgency (*act now*). Without it, you risk no decision, price pressure, and losses to competitors who make a defensible case for better impact than you.

And you need to summarize it in a one-line mission statement, so everyone is on the same page about exactly what the initiative is. When the mission is fuzzy you risk indecision with stakeholders at odds over what to do.

Here are two real examples, both redacted and slightly changed to protect anonymity.

The first blueprint was one built by a client in a RAIN Group workshop for an opportunity he was working on (and presented and won the sale the next week).

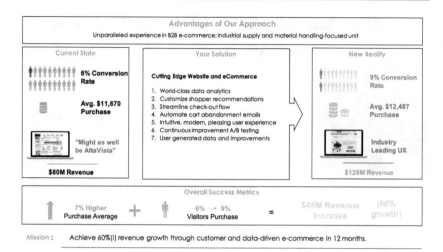

FIGURE 7.3 Buyer Change Blueprint, Example #1

The second blueprint was built for a RAIN Group client.

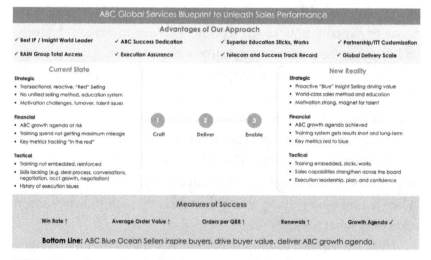

FIGURE 7.4 Buyer Change Blueprint, Example #2

A common challenge we hear is that it's difficult to summarize everything on one page, especially for large engagements. In fact, that's when it's most important. The more complex something is, the more important it is to summarize it in plain language on one page.

Making the New Reality Case for Change on a Page in a Virtual World

Making the new reality case, whether face-to-face or virtual, makes a huge difference in client success. The advantage in virtual selling is this: It's *easier to collaborate* with buyers to build it virtually than it is to do it live.

While face-to-face selling has the advantage of people being in a room, once people plug in computers and start sharing presentations, it often doesn't seem like it's connecting to buyers. Sellers must learn the nuances of delivering live presentations so they don't bore their buyers, don't drone on, and don't lose the chance to make the right connections with people through their presentation and stories.

In virtual selling, screen sharing and presenting are more natural. Story-building and storytelling with visuals that unfold as the seller speaks are much more natural online.

In the next chapter, we describe the storytelling component of building your new reality change case, both early in the sale to drive new priorities and approaches, and later in the sale to bring the whole story together in finalist presentations and proposals.

After that, we back up a bit and talk about how to develop the meat of the story in collaboration with your buyers.

Chapter 7 Key Takeaways

- **If a seller's job is to drive change,** a virtual seller needs to focus on building a case by collaborating with buyers, drawing them into the process and creating a blueprint that captures the case for change on a single page.

- **Virtual sellers can impress buyers when:**
  - The change blueprint is developed together with the buyer
  - The case for change is clear and rational
  - The case follows the blueprint that represents:
  - Priorities: "Do this, not that"
    - Approaches: "This way, not that"
    - Impact: "Because"
    - Decisions: "Act now, not later"
    - Partners: "With us, not them"

SECTION III:

LEADING SPECIALTY AND ADVANCED VIRTUAL CONVERSATIONS

In our *What Sales Winners Do Differently* research, we learned that sellers that win major sales do the following most differently than the sellers that come in the closest second place, but ultimately, lose.

Sellers that win:

- **Connect:** They build relationships with people, and connect the dots well between needs and solutions.
- **Convince:** They make the case for change persuasively.
- **Collaborate:** They collaborate with buyers, working with them highly interactively in the selling process.

In the previous chapters, we covered much of "connect" and the building blocks of "convince." In the next several chapters, we continue covering how sellers convince and persuade, and do so through a balance of interacting with buyers deeply, collaborating throughout the sales process, and when it's time to present, doing so persuasively.

This area is especially challenging in virtual selling, and especially different, because of a concept we'll cover shortly called functional fixedness. Essentially, buyers think of the virtual world and virtual meetings as place where people present to them. And sellers think the same, virtual meetings are places to present, so they talk and present, talk and present, and bore the life out of deeply disengaged buyers.

When sellers figure out virtual collaboration, shift to a much more interactive style, and are able to hold buyer engagement when they do present by structuring their presentations as stories, they become exceptionally persuasive and effective.

CHAPTER 8

INSPIRING BUYERS WITH NEW IDEAS VIRTUALLY

THE *I* IN RAIN SELLING DOUBLES AS A REMINDER TO DRIVE INSIGHT.

To learn more about RAIN Selling, visit the *Virtual Selling* book tools on the RAIN Group website for free content (http://raingrp.com/VS-BookTools), or pick up a copy of the *Wall Street Journal* bestselling book, *Rainmaking Conversations.*

Telling a Convincing Story

con•vince /kən'vins/

1. Cause (someone) to believe firmly in the truth of something.
2. Persuade (someone) to take action.

Building confidence in the validity of an idea. Inspiring action. When sellers can inspire buyers with ideas, we call this insight selling.

The sellers who are most capable of insight selling sell the most.

While some sellers are naturals at insight selling, whether virtually or in person, many struggle with it. Sellers might know with great certainty that when buyers buy from them the buyer will be better off as a result, but they just can't get the *buyers* to believe it.

What's interesting, though, is that both the sellers who are good at selling an idea and those who aren't, often each understand the idea and its importance. It's just that the good ones communicate it far better than others.

On the one hand, selling virtually makes communicating ideas and inspiring action more difficult. Yet, it also provides unique opportunities that allow you to distinguish yourself from unskilled sellers.

Those who do sell ideas well—whether they know it or not—often satisfy the same storytelling criteria and follow the same basic format. The great thing? The structure is *simple, learnable,* and *lends itself to virtual selling*. In many ways, this format shines brightly in a virtual environment, where sellers can make use of the many tools at their fingertips to engage buyers and bring them on a powerful journey, one that leaves buyers saying, "I want that for us and I believe, together, we can all make it happen!"

This storytelling format, the structure of persuasive presentations, is called a Convincing Story.

The underlying structure of a Convincing Story looks like Figure 8.1. (For a downloadable PDF visit http://raingrp.com/VS-BookTools.)

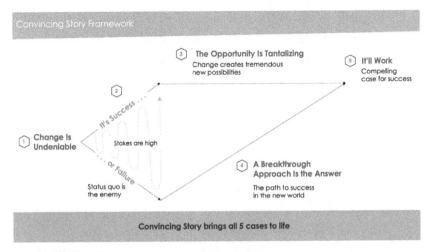

FIGURE 8.1 Convincing Story Framework

The five key components of the Convincing Story are:

1. **Change Is Undeniable:** Build rapport and establish credibility by demonstrating keen insight into the buyer's world, and set up the need for the buyer—the hero of the story—to change because their world has changed. The change can be external (e.g., industry, economy, buyer preferences, competition) or internal (e.g., a change of CEO).

   Regardless, the change will drive new changes that need to happen.

2. **It's Success or Failure:** Next, establish the current state and why it's not good enough and it will lead to ever-increasing failure. By establishing the current state and why it will lead to failure, you give the hero's adversary a name: the status quo.

   The leading indicators that the status quo will ultimately result in failure can be anything: lack of results, slipping market share, wasted time on workarounds, ideas whose time has passed—anything. Things might not even be that bad, but the status quo will still lead to failure. Imagine it's 1909 and you run the most successful horse-trading dealership in Detroit.

Regardless of how good it may be *at that moment in time*, staying the same will not lead to much of a future.

The masters at virtual insight selling not only show buyers what to run toward, but also give them something to run away from.

Your ability to establish the fact that success is available to the buyer is critical. Average sellers focus too early on establishing the "this way… not that" path. These are *how* messages. Such messages are important, but only after you establish "do this… not that" or the priority to act or change in the first place. The *why* message must come first.

Getting to the new reality—the place where buyers are achieving the results they want—is the why. And why is a powerful force. Simply suggesting, "Here's where we are and it isn't good enough," isn't, well, good enough. It's incomplete. It doesn't create the intense feeling of desire that's so important for change, and so critical for selling success.

3. **The Opportunity Is Tantalizing:** Communicate excitement around new possibilities. Many virtual sellers believe they know how to tell a ROI story. In fact, our research showed that sellers ranked "making the ROI case clear to buyers" at the very bottom of the list of challenges they face when virtual selling.

But remember, 84 percent of buyers said sellers weren't very effective doing this in remote or virtual interactions. Communicating the opportunity in ROI terms was the skill sellers displayed the least effectively when selling to buyers.

Later in the sales process, sellers should customize the ROI story to the client. But early in the sale, it's important to establish the significant opportunity available to those who are willing to act. As you do this, continue to point out how others have tried to achieve here and failed. Buyers will often say afterwards (or think it, even if they don't say it out loud), "That was us. We tried and failed, too."

4. **A Breakthrough Approach Is the Answer:** Just when the buyer feels resigned to failure, you show them a *different* path. "This way... not that!" When they see that others have achieved what they haven't, they'll feel a very powerful emotion: envy. They'll want what others have that they don't.

   But still, making the change a reality is not necessarily a slam dunk. If it were easy, everyone would do it. Since, however, this is what you help people do—and what you have a track record of doing—you can guide them around the many pitfalls that can get in the way.

   This not only establishes you as a scarce and differentiated solution ("this way, not that... with us, not them"), but also as a straight shooter who's on their side. Do so and buyers start to believe you and trust you—and the solution—that much more. Some sellers get this far but miss out on convincing the buyer they have the special sauces necessary to achieve the possible outcomes. When buyers don't know why they need you, they understand the ROI case is compelling, but they think they can achieve it without you. An outcome of masterful virtual selling is to help the buyer see that your knowledge, collaboration, and partnership in the journey is essential for their success.

5. **It'll Work:** Collaborate for action. Most sellers recommend action, specifically a next step. Few, however, build in collaboration. When buyers feel like sellers collaborate with them, they are much more likely to buy, and to buy from that particular seller. At this point, your call to action will be to invite discussion and collaboration.

   Whether you are early or late in the sale, you want to invite collaboration. Collaboration involves including the buyer in the story. When people are involved in something, they become invested in its success. The more they become invested in something, the more they take ownership in seeing it through.

Perhaps most powerfully, collaboration creates shared experience. Shared experience leads to real intimacy. Intimacy is a pillar of trust. And trust is essential when building confidence and selling an idea.

So, there you have it: the five components of a Convincing Story. Simple. Learnable. Powerful.

Use the Convincing Story structure and you'll achieve three outcomes with buyers that you need in order to sell an idea: learn, feel, do.

Learn

- Current state is not good enough. It needs to change.
- You "get it" and "get them" because, without much interaction, you have already described their world.
- The possible new reality is much more desirable. The stakes are high if you can win this game.
- The rational impact (the ROI) is clear.
- There's a path to get there, but it requires different thinking and action.
- Do it right to achieve results.

Feel

- The depth of how undesirable their current state is (e.g., frustrations, problems, and difficulties).
- The full desirability of the possible new reality and everything that comes with it, including money, success, attention, relief, happiness, even envy of those who have what the buyer doesn't.
- Confidence that you, your offerings, and your company can help them achieve results.

- Confidence that the result is achievable and, at the same time, worth the risk.

Do: Collaborate with you to bring the new reality to life.

Differences in Telling a Convincing Story— Face-to-Face vs. Virtual Selling

A Convincing Story is the narrative flow for making a case. Consider how Convincing Stories rank on the Virtual Selling Divergence Scale, a measure of how different selling is when comparing face-to-face vs. virtual selling.

1. Not that much different
2. A little different
3. Somewhat different
4. Different
5. Significantly different

Convincing Story, a key component of case-making, is a **5 out of 5 different**. It's significantly different. Here's how.

Component	Face-to-Face	Virtual Selling
Early in the sale	Live face-to-face with presentations and white boards, and on the phone with voice only, to establish the possible new reality	Live on video with screen share; naturally with story-in-motion on screens; harder to gain and maintain attention; easier to white board and annotate

Component	Face-to-Face	Virtual Selling
Late in the sale	Live proposal presentations with full-sensory experience	Voice, video, and screen only; more challenging to make a full-sensory experience, more impressive to buyers when sellers *actually achieve it*

Convincing Story in a Virtual Selling World

Sellers use the Convincing Story framework both early and late in the sales process:

- **Early—Priorities and Approaches:** At first, buyers need to know that something new and different to them is even possible. They need to be *introduced* to and excited by an idea. This works to both help buyers set new priorities ("do this... not that") and to inspire them to tackle priorities—new or existing—through different approaches ("this way... not that").

- **Late—All Case-Making:** Later in the sales process, buyers need all five cases (priorities, approaches, impact, decisions, and partners) in order to move forward with a purchase that falls in the seller's favor. These cases all come together in one Convincing Story.

Convincing Story Examples and Tips

Perhaps some of the most impressive sellers, trained or not, are entrepreneurs who raise investment capital. Corporate sales people often sell an idea, but entrepreneurs literally sell *an idea*. Even before anything else exists.

The examples that follow show a mix of sales presentations—some corporate some fundraising—that exemplify points in the Convincing Story framework.

1. Change Is Undeniable

Great sales stories start with **Change Is Undeniable.**

The Analog to Digital Transformation

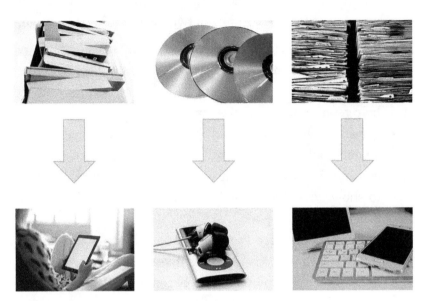

FIGURE 8.2 Convincing Story, Change Is Undeniable

Take this example from Canvas, a company that replaces paper-based processes with mobile apps and forms. This is the opening to the deck that helped them raise $9 million in venture capital.[1]

The point is fairly straightforward: These things are happening, and there's no denying it. The visual, which is not a sophisticated graphic design, can be recreated by sellers with a minimum knowledge of PowerPoint, Prezi, Keynote, Slidebean, or Google Slides skills. It's oldthingpicture, arrow, newthingpicture.

With a little voiceover by the seller, it draws an audience into world of the story. This is what you want to do, too.

As a seller, you may be saying, "But I'm not selling an app, I'm selling accounting services," or financial services, technology hardware, consumer goods to stores, engineering services, industrial materials, and so on.

Regardless of what you're selling, the question to ask yourself is this: Is it more difficult for your clients to succeed now compared to fifteen, five, or even two years ago? For example:

- Accounting services selling to retail companies: Retail profit margins have dropped 32 percent over the past five years. (Story can go on to tell company how accounting firm can help retail companies raise margins.)
- Consumer goods: Ten years ago, more than 17 percent of consumers looked up new products on the internet before purchasing them; last year it was 74 percent. (Story can go on to show how in-store internet searches can result in greater purchases.)
- Industrial materials: Products marketed as sustainable grew 560 percent faster than those that were not. (Story can go on to show how a company can become legitimately sustainable with their materials at the same as their current rate of expenditure.)

Will all your storytelling open with ideas as impressive as these? Perhaps not. But the undeniable change you highlight can be more mundane, as long as it opens the door to the buyer setting a new priority for action. Here's an email example from an accounting firm that generated a significant amount of additional revenue with custom outreach to their clients, executed almost exclusively virtually.

Hi «CLIENT»,

«RAPPORT CHECK IN.»

Quick thought: In the last two years the IRS has reviewed dozens of cases of companies that have claimed the research and development tax credit. What they've accepted has broadened enough that I think it's possible you might qualify. If you do, it could save you north of $50k in taxes annually.

Are you up for discussing it?

Looking forward to catching up soon.

«NAME»

ALTERNATIVE OPENING— CHALLENGE AND OPPORTUNITY

The classic opening to an idea presentation is the simple challenge and opportunity. Certainly, you can open with this, and it can be effective, but to the extent you can highlight a major change that has opened a new door to a new possibility, your story becomes more compelling.

If you include the challenge and opportunity concept in your story, it's still better to put it just after the Change Is Undeniable opening.

We include this here because many sellers have trouble seeing that *change* applies to what they sell. Sometimes they're right, but most of the time, with a little thinking, there's an undeniable change they can share with buyers that begins with a story and ends with a purchase.

2. It's Success or Failure

The idea is that the change will not just create a group of "haves" and "have nots" but, rather, separate people into one of two camps—success or failure. Here's an adaptation of a presentation by Mixpanel used to raise $65 million.[2]

PROBLEM 1

Most of the world will make decisions by either guessing or using their gut. They will be either lucky or wrong.

FIGURE 8.3 Convincing Story, Success or Failure, Problem 1

PROBLEM 2

Companies on mobile & web are measuring bullshit metrics like page views and installs. It's really hard to be really sophisticated.

FIGURE 8.4 Convincing Story, Success or Failure, Problem 2

This directly sets up the point that people who make decisions based on guesses or their guts are shooting in the dark, giving themselves a great chance to be wrong. And even people who think they are using analytics to inform decisions, in fact, are not.

With simple clarity, the presentation continues to say that because they solved the problem, they (and their customers) are winners.

COMPETITIVE ADVANTAGE
In 2010, we built the most sophisticated analytics database engine to answer questions that existing technology could not answer. It's the reason we are winning.

FIGURE 8.5 Convincing Story, Success or Failure, Problem 3

The implication is, if the investors fund them, they will win, too.

3. The Opportunity Is Tantalizing

Here's an example from a company called Front.

THE OPPORTUNITY

Slack proved that businesses are ready to buy good communication tools. They're going after the internal communications market.

We're going after the bigger opportunity.
Front will own the external communications space.

FIGURE 8.6 The Opportunity Is Tantalizing

Front compares its opportunity as greater than Slack's. As of this writing, Slack's market capitalization was $14.7 billion, a return most investors would be pleased to yield.

Of course, it's unlikely you're pitching investors to get capital. Probably your job is to sell an existing product, service, or capability. This is good, because for established companies, establishing the tantalizing opportunity is more straightforward: You share actual results.

Here's a simple slide of ours that we often use to demonstrate the effectiveness of the Execution Assurance coaching we pioneered to make sure sales training actually drives change and results.

FIGURE 8.7 The Opportunity Is Tantalizing, Demonstrating Effectiveness

During our sales conversations, we note that leaders at each one of these companies is available to speak to buyers to learn about how it worked (which foreshadows point #5 of the Convincing Story, "It'll work").

The purpose here is not yet to establish the belief that it'll work. It's okay at this point if buyers are skeptical. You might even leave off client logos connected to results like this until later.

- **Improved number of deals closed** year-over-year by 15.2%

- **Gross profit margin on sales won improved by 12.2%**

- **Reduced average days** to close by 10.4%

- Results were so impressive we won a prestigious Stevie Award for **Sales Training/Coaching Program of the Year**

FIGURE 8.8 The Opportunity Is Tantalizing, How It Has Worked

In fact, you *want* buyers to have a sense that the potential results push the edge of what's possible, because of something known as the anchoring effect.

If you set an achievement target a buyer might think is barely plausible, say 100 percent improvement in X, you set what becomes an unconscious stretch possibility target in the mind of the buyer. Then, later in the decision process when you build belief that the target is achievable, buyers will make the argument to themselves and others: "Even if we can achieve just one-third of this given the investment and time, and even if it takes twice as long, it will still be a huge success."

But first, buyers have to get over the hump of why they haven't achieved it yet. They have to *begin to believe* that it's possible.

4. A Breakthrough Approach Is the Answer

Let's look at a totally different type of example. The diet and weight loss industry, with many great successes, has failure rates that can challenge buyer belief in any given program. Recently, we saw Weight Watchers make a bold brand change to redefine itself as WW, with more of an emphasis on overall wellness and less on shedding pounds. To the prospective buyer, WW would appear to be deeper, more focused on mindset, and a connection to a healthy lifestyle. Why is this important? Because it's different, and a breakthrough approach less likely to be compared to past failures.

When buyers are presented with a new way of thinking, they begin to hope that past failures won't repeat themselves. To build a buyer's confidence, the approach has to be different enough to lead the buyer to believe a different outcome is in the offing. You do that when you establish your "this way... not that" case solidly.

What follows here depends on your offering and your stage in the sales process. Early in the process you might want a few slides to show how what you do stands out from the typical approach. Later in the sales process, you will probably want to outline the specific approach you've crafted for this customer.

5. It'll Work

We at RAIN Group once performed a loss analysis (sales opportunity, not weight) for one of our clients. Our client told us, "The ROI for this prospect would have been 25X achieved in just six months. I don't know why they didn't see it."

When we asked the client's prospect they said, "Oh I saw it. I got it. I would have liked to achieve it. But I didn't believe it would come true. If I did, I would have signed."

In our experience, not building buyer belief that something will work—the substantiation part of the value proposition we outlined in Chapter 2—is a huge reason sellers lose to "no decision" and, as well, lose to the competition, especially when their prices are higher or they are trying to unseat an incumbent.

It's the fear of failure, the risk, that concerns the buyer, not the reward.

To combat this early in the sale, have the following at the ready:

- Case studies with named buyers
- Testimonial letters and videos with named results

The names are important. We at RAIN Group have a case study that shows Bright Horizons Family Solutions increased its average size of sale by 38 percent. When one of our consultants mention this, they often navigate to the two-minute video where the client shares these results.

FIGURE 8.9 It'll Work, Statistics

Not only is it more natural for you to open a website or video in a virtual environment when you're already on the computer, but it helps to maintain the engagement threshold with the introduction of different and interesting media.

If you don't have named case studies, or if you're selling something totally new to the market, it's even more important for you to make a strong case. This might mean using:

- Case studies without names
- Demonstrations and explainers of how what you do works and produces results, or will if certain conditions are met
- Willingness of your current or past clients and customers to act as references for you.

If you want to inspire a buyer to consider a new idea when you are selling virtually—to set a new priority or change approaches—use the Convincing Story as the framework to make your case.

Chapter 8 Key Takeaways

- **A Convincing Story** is the narrative flow for making any case. Its basic structure is simple, learnable, and lends itself to virtual selling.

- **Developing a balanced rational/emotional response** in a virtual setting takes planning. Craft every Convincing Story to lead to **well-planned** answers to the following questions:
  - What do I want them to learn?
  - What do I want them to feel?
  - What do I want them to do?

- **The five components** of the Convincing Story are:
  1. Change is undeniable: where great sales stories start.
  2. It's success or failure: the premise that change will divide everyone into haves and have nots.
  3. The opportunity is tantalizing: inspiring buyers to believe that reaching a compelling goal is possible.
  4. A breakthrough approach is the answer: presenting buyers with a new way of thinking.
  5. It'll work: building buyer belief that the new idea will actually work.

CHAPTER 9

DELIVERING POWERFUL VIRTUAL PROPOSAL PRESENTATIONS

To learn more about RAIN Selling, visit the *Virtual Selling* book tools on the RAIN Group website for free content (http://raingrp. com/VS-BookTools), or pick up a copy of the *Wall Street Journal* bestselling book, *Rainmaking Conversations*.

Organize and Orchestrate

Too many late-stage sales presentations—face-to-face and virtual—land with a thud. We've had the opportunity to speak with hundreds of clients, observe late-stage sales and proposal presentations, and hear directly from thousands of buyers over the years through the RAIN Group Center for Sales Research. This is what we typically see and hear:

Seller is not focused enough on the buyer

- Seller didn't inspire confidence in the seller's company
- Seller didn't inspire confidence in the seller's offering
- Seller didn't inspire confidence in the seller themselves
- None of the solutions or selling teams really stood out
- Buyer is not convinced that changing what they're doing is worth the effort at all

There are two ways virtual sellers can take the lead and flip this on its head: 1) improve structure and 2) deliver proposals and presentations in the form of a story to maximize chances that buyers take action, now, with you.

In Buyers' Brains

Daniel Kahneman won the Nobel Prize in economics in 2002 for his analysis on why buyers don't make decisions rationally. He and his colleague, Amos Tversky, discovered some surprising facts about how people make decisions.[1]

1. People don't make decisions based on actual value. They make decisions based more on subjective perceived value.
2. Buyers evaluate investments relative to reference points, typically related to what they've experienced before or what their perception of something is.
3. People view any improvements related to this reference point as gains, and any shortcomings as losses.
4. Most importantly, losses are perceived by buyers to have a much greater impact than gains.

Here's how applying these principles as you organize and orchestrate your late-stage proposal and proposal presentations will help put you over the top.

Topic	Where sellers often fail	Where sellers can succeed
Perceived value	• Templated or barely customized offers that focus on product • Flat and un-orchestrated presentations that leave buyers feeling lack of focus and effort from sellers shapes perception of low vendor partnership and potential gains after purchase • Minimal investment of time in relationship lowers perceived value of overall purchase	• Customer-focused proposals based on real need, real impact, and full value story • Engaging, tight communications help build confidence and trust. Obvious level of effort in proposing solutions showcases value of partnership and likely client result achievement • Increased connection to seller and people in seller organizations strengthens overall value perception
Reference points	• Lack of specificity in needs discovery and data gathering leads to generalized demonstrations and incorrect assumptions leading to lack of confidence in seller	• Clear understanding of current state, issues, and data leads to specific, engaging, customer-focused presentations that inspire connection, trust, and belief in sellers

Topic	Where sellers often fail	Where sellers can succeed
Gains and losses in relation to reference points	• Lack of reference point knowledge denies buyers a clear understanding of what they are diverging from • Because buyers don't see enough difference, they are more likely to stick with the status quo (seller loses to no decision or incumbent) or change only gradually (buy a lesser offering or decrease their investment)	• Strong current state knowledge leads to ability to make gain and loss comparisons that are accurate, and that are both desirable enough to change and plausible • Buyers see the great difference compared to their reference points, want to change, and are more willing to invest properly to achieve the potential returns
Psychological impact of losses	• Seller's belief in their offerings and capabilities much stronger than buyer's belief in same • Focusing too much on generalized ROI, failing to make it real by showing concrete, specific results that seller can help buyer achieve	• Seller understands that buyer will need to make a great leap to change from status quo; organizes story to make that leap inevitable • Focusing on actual ROI from current state, taking into account likely losses of inaction (staying with status quo), or choosing the right approach and path forward

In face-to-face selling, when sellers show up at a buyer site, deliver at least a good presentation of their proposal, and handle Q&A in person with buyers, they can often overcome some of the issues here and impress buyers. But in the 2D world of virtual selling, it's much more challenging to get over these humps. Sellers tell us that even if they want to go all out to get the sale, they don't know what to do.

Here's what to do.

Sell the Change with the Right Structure and Delivery for a Virtual Setting

The combination of the Convincing Story and the Buyer Change Blueprint are the keys to building a presentation that will help you sell the change your solution delivers. In the virtual 2D world, you can't rely on the organic connections that develop between people in the same room. It's much harder in the virtual medium due to the higher threshold to grab attention and maintain engagement.

Therefore, use the strong structure outlined in the previous chapter, the Convincing Story.

Convincing Story Framework

1. Change is undeniable.
2. It's success or failure.
3. The opportunity is tantalizing.
4. A breakthrough approach is the answer.
5. It'll work.

How you build the Convincing Story and deliver it for a virtual proposal presentation is different, however, than how you do it when you're opening buyers' minds to new ideas and possibilities.

Differences in Telling a Convincing Story— Face-to-Face vs. Virtual Selling

Telling a Convincing Story is the narrative flow for making any case. Consider how Convincing Stories rank on the Virtual Selling Divergence Scale, a measure of how different a component of selling is when comparing face-to-face vs. virtual selling.

1. Not that much different
2. A little different
3. Somewhat different
4. Different
5. Significantly different

The Convincing Story, a key component of case-making, is a **5 out of 5 different**. It's significantly different. Here's how.

Component	Face-to-Face	Virtual Selling
Meeting Dynamics	Live meetings enable more reading of the room, and easier emotional connectivity	Requires frequent check-ins and better building of story structure via media with planned stops for conversation points
Buyer Mindset	Buyers in face-to-face meetings, especially later stage where the consideration set of sellers is narrower, will be more focused	Like other points in the sales process fatigue sets in earlier in the meeting, thus presentations need to change to become more interactive, more like conversations
Case-making	Can flow in conversation and with proper structure, but also runs the risk of getting lost in sidetracked conversations and live banter	Can be done with great effect using Convincing Story and Buyer Change Blueprint structure and approach

As you read through this chapter, note that we separate out thoughts on structure and delivery. For delivery, we are assuming a sixty-minute timeframe. If you have ninety minutes or longer you should adjust, taking care to add in interaction and conversation if you get more time on the clock (a *seven more* presentation is likely to result in lost buyer attention).

Meanwhile, here's a place to start for timings:

- Introductions: five minutes
- Convincing Story as outlined below: thirty to forty minutes total delivered *interactively with discussion throughout*:
  a. Introduction and Current State/New Reality: ten minutes
  b. Your Solution for Change: ten minutes
  c. Impact: ROI Case five minutes
  d. Why Now: Urgency Case: five minutes
  e. Why Us: five minutes
- Buyer Change Blueprint Summary: five minutes
- Question and Answer: fifteen to twenty-five minutes

STRUCTURE:

Change is undeniable.
Open with change that *has happened to the buyer*. This could be anything you learned during the sales process that is material to the situation. For example:

- Two years ago, the organization was growing at a rate of 15 percent, this has now slowed to 5 percent.
- Competitor X has come on strong and is growing at a rate of 17 percent.
- Jane Smith took over four months ago as CEO, and set a new, ambitious change goal of X.
- Undesirable staff turnover has increased 31 percent in the last eighteen months.

- Your supply chain has grown recently from thirty-one raw materials to 155.

This opening is effective using either one major change, or perhaps three changes combined that summarize why you're all meeting. By talking immediately about *them* not about *you*, you draw them into the world of your story.

Visual Example:

FIGURE 9.1 Change Is Undeniable

DELIVERY:

It's success or failure.
Demonstrate that it's success or failure—there's no middle ground anymore.

- Remind everyone what's not working and why.
- Make sure the status quo is obviously the enemy.
- Begin positioning for how you can help in a unique way.

ABC Global Services Blueprint to Unleash Sales Performance

Current State

Strategic

- Transactional, reactive, "Red" selling
- No unified selling method, education system
- Motivation challenges, turnover, talent issues

Financial

- ABC growth agenda at risk
- Training spend not getting maximum mileage
- Key metrics tracking "in the red"

Tactical

- Training not embedded, reinforced
- Skills lacking (e.g., deal process, conversations, negotiation, acct growth)
- History of execution issues

FIGURE 9.2 Buyer Change Blueprint, Current State

Now is where you begin to incorporate the Buyer Change Blueprint. The most powerful way we've seen to demonstrate known issues is to clearly share them in a window listed in a left-hand Current State column, and then initiate the conversation. (See Figure 9.2 Buyer Change Blueprint, Current State.)

Don't avoid talking about sticky problems, what hasn't worked, or lack of results. Talk about them. Remind them of past failures (with tact—people may be quite sensitive, squirmy, and defensive at this point).

By doing this, you set the reference point—the place they want to be *different than*. Many sellers talk about benefits and ROI, but without the reference point, buyers are not clear about what they are diverging *from*. The Buyer Change Blueprint helps you set that reference point with clarity.

Note that we haven't highlighted specific financial reference points yet. This is by design as our goal is to set the emotional stage before we get to the rational stage. The ROI case comes later. Meanwhile, the next step is to juxtapose the potential future state with the current state. (See Figure 9.3 Buyer Change Blueprint, New Reality.)

Again, it's success or failure. By stating in qualitative terms what will be different, you affect all Kahneman's decision-making points:

- Perceived value goes up. The actual value is the ROI case, but if we just posited the ROI case here in this example, it would not have nearly the impact than when it is couched in the full, pent-up-with-emotions picture.
- Reference points become clear, and specific to their situation. You paint the before-and-after picture *for them*. Powerfully and simply.
- You set the picture of the gains available as they face mounting losses that you highlight for them, tactfully.

ABC Global Services Blueprint to Unleash Sales Performance

Current State

Strategic
- Transactional, reactive, "Red" selling
- No unified selling method, education system
- Motivation challenges, turnover, talent issues

Financial
- ABC growth agenda at risk
- Training spend not getting maximum mileage
- Key metrics tracking "in the red"

Tactical
- Training not embedded, reinforced
- Skills lacking (e.g., deal process, conversations, negotiation, acct growth)
- History of execution issues

New Reality

Strategic
- Proactive "Blue" Insight Selling driving value
- World-class sales method and education
- Motivation strong, magnet for talent

Financial
- ABC growth agenda achieved
- Training system gets results short and long-term
- Key metrics red to blue

Tactical
- Training embedded, sticks, works
- Sales capabilities strengthen across the board
- Execution leadership, plan, and confidence

FIGURE 9.3 Buyer Change Blueprint, New Reality

- By positioning growth agenda at risk, with the CEO telling the board sales performance is untenable, everyone knows the losses at stake (in this case, their jobs).

Note that the positioning might be different if you were presenting to an owner of a business: that person's job may not be at risk, but their future dreams may be. You need to position the loss that's important for the consumers of the presentation. Knowing what people care about is not the same from person to person and role to role.

A Convincing Story is an emotional journey, often quite a roller coaster. The net effect is that the buyer feels how high the stakes are by being reminded that they are trapped and need to get out. At the same time, you'll clarify for them how they can achieve a new reality they desire.

Also, as a delivery tip, it's best to build the presentation content-block by content-block, weaving back and forth between the current state and the new reality. In this case, you'd deliver the three strategic bullets on the left, then talk about what they could be in the new reality, by unveiling the three points on the right.

Then you'd unveil the three financial points on the left, weaving back to the "negative" current state, and then over to the right by delivering the financial points in the new reality. Then tactical left, and tactical right.

The concept is called dissatisfaction layering. By going back and forth between the painful current state and the desirable new reality, you not only establish a very important rational gap (you're here, but you could and should be there), but also maximize the negative feelings associated with being in the undesirable place.

The opportunity is tantalizing.
This is the place for the ROI case. Most people think this is the meat of the story, but it's just part of it. As Kahneman argues and our research confirms, people make decisions based on subjective,

perceived value. More people will be excited about the emotional benefits of the new reality case than the financials, but keep in mind, the financials help buyers justify their emotional reactions.

Indeed, many people who are economically oriented will have a very strong emotional attachment to the ROI case itself, but by and large, it's best to balance making the whole case—emotional and rational—as a complete story.

Meanwhile, if the buyers were to move forward in our example, they would achieve a tantalizing ROI. A 27.9 times return on investment, including all costs, compared to the margin that would be generated from the investment. Some psychological studies point to the need to show at least a ten-times return for buyers to act; 27.9 times is a lot better than that. (See Figure 9.4 The Opportunity Is Tantalizing.)

A breakthrough approach is the answer.

Now that you have the impact case clearly laid out (and plugged into the Buyer Change Blueprint), here's where you present your breakthrough approach, the approach that will bridge the gap between the current state and the new reality. (See Figure 9.5 Buyer Change Blueprint, Breakthrough Approach.)

In this example, following the rule of three, there are three stages of the breakthrough approach that will bridge the gap.

For a proposal presentation, we recommend having three slides in the middle describing your approach. As you deliver, build each one of them to keep the visual interest; presentation watchers will want to know what comes up with each click as the content appears.

The proposal that you submit may be longer than this, and may contain appendices with technical detail, but if you only have ten or fifteen minutes, building three slides will fill that time. Many sellers fall into the trap of too many slides detailing their offerings, and then run out of time for discussion.

It'll work.

Bridging the gap between *A breakthrough approach* and *It'll work* is information about you as a partner and why you're not just the right *approach* but the right *company* and *team* to help make sure everything comes together for success. (See Figure 9.6 Why Us.)

Importantly, you make the "with us" case not just by what you outline, but by what you do.

Buyers often buy from the seller who impresses them most. When you lead the sales process the right way, customize your proposal presentation delivery, and show how you'll be the best and most customer-focused partner for them, they'll notice.

USE VIDEO

Here are two powerful ideas that lend themselves to virtual selling to help you stand out:

- **Personalized Buyer Testimonial:** To continue to build confidence that success will be achieved in the "It'll work" section, consider asking a customer of yours to provide a one-minute video testimonial just for this sale. When a buyer's peer sings your praises directly to them it's both engaging and confidence-inspiring.
- **Team Video:** Let's say seven people on your team will work on the buyer engagement. Have all seven people introduce themselves, say what they do, and say something special about why they're very much looking forward to working with the buyer. This can take a minute or so as well.

These techniques are both engaging and confidence-inspiring, and bring the personal touch to a 2D virtual delivery.

You might simply say, "We'll make your success our mission." They will believe or not believe that, based on how you have comported yourself throughout the sales process. You'll reinforce your

Improve Key Metrics across 600 QBRs

Why Act

	Before	Δ	After	Accretive $ ↑	Why
Orders per QBR	6.75	↑ 5%	7.1	$36.4m	Increased pipeline with insight training, acct planning, XP Challenge
Avg. order value	$180k	↑ 5%	$189k	$36.4m	Stronger differentiation, relationships, perception of value decreases discounting
Sales cycle in 2,025 opps	12 month	↓ 8.3%	11 month	$30.2m	Better qualification, stronger value prop (especially Why Now), XP Challenge
Win rate	27%	↑ 10%	29.7%	$72.9m	Stronger value prop development and communication, stronger relationships
Renewals	$972m	↑ 5%	$1.2bn	$60.7m	Stronger value prop of seller and ABC solution, decreased acct team turnover
Total				**$251.64m**	
Contribution margin @ 40%				$100.5m	
Initiative investment				$3.6m	

ROI | 27.9 X in accretive margin

Assumptions

- 600 quota bearing reps(QBR)
- $180k avg SOV (NCV)
- Contribution margin of 40%
- 170 sales mgrs and 1,000 specialists share targets with QBRs; avoided double counting
- Investment in RG $2.3m, internal ABC costs $1.3m estimated (e.g. travel)

Drive Strategic Imperatives

✓ Enormous untapped potential in accounts; leaving $ on the table

✓ ABC growth agenda at great risk

✓ Increase seller retention

✓ Decrease ramp up time

✓ Install world-class across-the-board sales, account, and mgt. method

✓ Attract world-class sellers

✓ Build customer first reputation of driving value

✓ Significant motivation and culture strengthening

FIGURE 9.4 The Opportunity Is Tantalizing

FIGURE 9.5 Buyer Change Blueprint, Breakthrough Approach

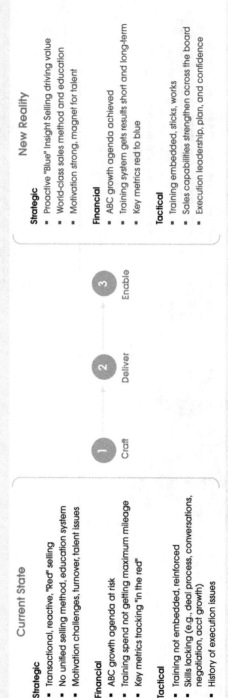

ABC Global Services Blueprint to Unleash Sales Performance

Current State

Strategic
- Transactional, reactive, "Red" selling
- No unified selling method, education system
- Motivation challenges, turnover, talent issues

Financial
- ABC growth agenda at risk
- Training spend not getting maximum mileage
- Key metrics tracking "in the red"

Tactical
- Training not embedded, reinforced
- Skills lacking (e.g., deal process, conversations, negotiation, acct growth)
- History of execution issues

1 Craft → **2** Deliver → **3** Enable

New Reality

Strategic
- Proactive "Blue" Insight Selling driving value
- World-class sales method and education
- Motivation strong, magnet for talent

Financial
- ABC growth agenda achieved
- Training system gets results short and long-term
- Key metrics red to blue

Tactical
- Training embedded, sticks, works
- Sales capabilities strengthen across the board
- Execution leadership, plan, and confidence

Measures of Success

Win Rate ↑ 2.7 PP   AOV ↑ $9k   Orders per QBR ↑ 5%   Renewals ↑ 5%   Growth Agenda ✓

Bottom Line: ABC Blue Ocean Sellers inspire buyers, drive value, deliver accretive $100m in margin this year.

174

intention by saying it—and bolster your words by including testimonial letters and videos, and case studies from other customers—but they'll judge the statement based on their experience with you thus far.

When you finish, you'll be left with a fully built Buyer Change Blueprint. A one-page summary that answers all the following:

- Why Act
- Why Now
- Why Us
- Why Trust

How the buyer answers the questions about their initiative overall, and their choice of partners and approaches, is what drives their decision. By structuring your proposal and presentation in this format, you make the decision easy for them: Act now... with you. (See Figure 9.7 Buyer Change Blueprint, Advantages of Our Approach.)

ADDITIONAL TIPS FOR PROPOSAL PRESENTATIONS

- If you don't know or haven't engaged all the stakeholders that might be at the finalist presentation, you can craft a five-minute survey to get their input beforehand. You can ask what is most important for them to hear, what they like to see in finalist presentations, any concerns they might have, what questions they want answered, and so on.

  Experienced sellers know the introductions slated to take five minutes can sometimes take twenty if the buyers all want to weigh in before you start the presentation. A pre-survey can save you this time, allow you to tailor the content and delivery, and sometimes most helpfully, get answered questions to individuals that you might not be able to cover at the presentation itself.

FIGURE 9.6 Why Us

Transformational Experience
Delivery | Service | Results

- We will make your success our mission
- Average delivery quality scores of 4.6 for program and 4.8 for facilitator
- Results with large B2B telecom, global insight delivery, complete sales education implementation, long-term large repeat clients
- Commitment to flexibility and customization; partnership is best path to success
- We will leverage what you have; if you have it, we won't build it
- Commitment to value-add and insight as we continue to work with you, including early access to all new RAIN Group Centre for Sales Research study results

IP and Research
Commitment to research-based thought leadership

- Insight Selling – we wrote the book: streamlined messaging approach works better
- Strategic and Key Account Management – top programs, impressive results, Top Performer database, SAM Competency Model, etc.
- RAIN Selling: Core consultative selling where needed for success fundamentals
- Winning Major Sales will drive win rate increases
- Prospecting, sales management and coaching, negotiation . . . all needed in the right places
- Extreme Sales Productivity Challenge – Watch activity and results soar

Education System
World-class education approach for learning to stick, work, and transfer to the job

- Top quality, up-to-date blended learning delivered in world-class extended enterprise LMS
- CRM integration embeds learning, drives behavior, and allows for strengthened results measurement
- Superior reinforcement approach and technologies (e.g., RAIN Mail, VILT, asynchronous lessons), and tracking and reporting capacities

Global Capabilities
8 offices, 70 full-time team members around the globe

- Delivered training in 75 countries
- Can deliver in multiple languages (will support translation of materials as needed)
- Expertise in sales process, leadership and change management, sales competency development
- Selling Power Magazine Top 20 Global Sales Training Firm 3 years running

ABC Global Services Blueprint to Unleash Sales Performance

Advantages of Our Approach

✓ Best IP / Insight World Leader   ✓ ABC Success Dedication   ✓ Superior Education Sticks, Works   ✓ Partnership/TTT Customization

✓ RAIN Group Total Access   ✓ Execution Assurance   ✓ Telecom and Success Track Record   ✓ Global Delivery Scale

Current State

Strategic
- Transactional, reactive, "Red" selling
- No unified selling method, education system
- Motivation challenges, turnover, talent issues

Financial
- ABC growth agenda at risk
- Training spend not getting maximum mileage
- Key metrics tracking "in the red"

Tactical
- Training not embedded, reinforced
- Skills lacking (e.g., deal process, conversations, negotiation, acct growth)
- History of execution issues

1 Craft   **2** Deliver   **3** Enable

New Reality

Strategic
- Proactive "Blue" Insight Selling driving value
- World-class sales method and education
- Motivation strong, magnet for talent

Financial
- ABC growth agenda achieved
- Training system gets results short and long-term
- Key metrics red to blue

Tactical
- Training embedded, sticks, works
- Sales capabilities strengthen across the board
- Execution leadership, plan, and confidence

Measures of Success

Win Rate ↑ 2.7 PP   AOV ↑ $9k   Orders per QBR ↑ 5%   Renewals ↑ 5%   Growth Agenda ✓

Bottom Line: ABC Blue Ocean Sellers inspire buvers. drive value. deliver accretive $100m in marain this vear.

FIGURE 9.7 Buyer Change Blueprint, Advantages of Our Approach

- Before the virtual presentation, send something physical to the buyers to add to the experience. These could be product samples, signed books, a walkthrough packet of materials, or even something to build hype.

FIGURE 9.8 Physical Mailing as Precursor to Virtual Meeting

- While the Buyer Change Blueprint and the Convincing Story framework are the keys to the structure of the delivery, make sure you attend to whatever else might be important for this particular presentation. Depending on your situation, it may be important to include common proposal items such as:
  - Responsibilities: stakeholders, who does what
  - Timeline: when will everything unfold

- ○ Fees
- ○ Key terms
- Satisfy specific buying criteria for this purchase (you may do that throughout, or you may summarize on a slide).
- Share your proposal with your champion (someone at the buyer company who you've connected with) beforehand to make sure you hit all the right notes. You can even record it as a presentation and send to them in advance.
- Record the presentation (with permission), edit for length, and send back to the buyers quickly. Editing it shows effort—for example, you might shorten ninety minutes down to forty-two. Editing also allows buyers to review what you talked about. And maybe share with someone who might need to see it but couldn't be there. You can also create an additional document or video that answers additional questions.
- Use an online document-sharing environment where you can track downloads, views, and other activity. Then you can see who's viewing what for the presentation, proposal, follow-up documents, and so on.

Chapter 9 Key Takeaways

- **Virtual presentations offer the opportunity** to differentiate yourself from the rest as you get deeper into the sales cycle. Use your tools, engagement approach, and the story format to your advantage.

- **Sell the change** with the right structure and delivery, by combining the Convincing Story and the Buyer Change Blueprint.

- **Begin talking immediately** about *them*, not you, and why the change they face is undeniable.

- **The co-creation of the blueprint** helps the buyer to agree on the case for change right now, with you, and frames your solution as the means to achieving a new desired reality. It is also incredibly powerful to conduct a virtual session where the buyer participates in developing the plan.

- **Show real results** to build buyer confidence.

CHAPTER 10

HOW TO COLLABORATE WITH BUYERS VIRTUALLY

To learn more about RAIN Selling, visit the *Virtual Selling* book tools on the RAIN Group website for free content (http://raingrp. com/VS-BookTools), or pick up a copy of the *Wall Street Journal* bestselling book, *Rainmaking Conversations.*

Power of Collaboration

Collaboration is an exceptionally powerful force behind the success of many top sellers, yet most sellers do not collaborate with buyers.

We'd like to be able to say, "In the past decade, sellers have gone from barely collaborating with buyers at all to collaborating most of the time. If you're not collaborating with buyers with rigor and skill, you will lose to all the sellers who are."

We can't say this, however, because the majority of sellers still do not collaborate with buyers.

So, you may not fail if you don't collaborate. But if you do collaborate, the opportunity to win more than everyone else is tantalizing.

Consider the following:

- According to 731 corporate decision-makers, "Collaborated with me" was the number two factor, of the forty-two studied, most separating sales winners of major sales from second-place finishers (second only to "Educated me on new ideas and perspectives)."[1]

- Top-performing sales negotiators were 2.6 times more likely to say "Approaches such as mutually brainstorming new ideas were used to build value" in actual sales negotiations.[2]
- Yet, according to corporate decision-makers, "Approaches such as mutually brainstorming new ideas and possibilities were used to build value" ranked seventeenth out of twenty-two factors (bottom quarter) that happened during a recent major sales negotiation.
- And when the rare seller did use "Approaches such as mutually brainstorming new ideas," a whopping 95 percent of decision-makers said doing this would make them more willing to negotiate with them again.
- Finally, top performers in strategic account management are 2.2 times more likely to "work collaboratively with «our» strategic accounts to co-create value in new, innovative ways."[3]

Collaboration works amazingly well in sales.

Recall from the previous chapter, Kahneman's arguments about how people make decisions.

Buying influence	How collaboration makes a difference
Decisions made on perceived vs. actual value	• Collaboration creates psychological ownership in the buyer that the initiative, and the solution, is *theirs*, not the seller's. • Collaboration deepens relationships by driving all areas of rapport, especially shared experience.

Buying influence	How collaboration makes a difference
Investments evaluated relative to reference points of past experience or perception	• When buyers find sellers to be collaborative, they view them as rare and special. • The sellers themselves become a positive force in the investment and value equation.
Improvements against reference points are gains, shortcomings are losses	• Collaboration is proven to change buyer perceptions, which changes the nature of the whole purchase itself, including unleashing actual, ROI-focused value unexpectedly. • Buyers see gains in what they will achieve. • When other sellers and their offerings add less value and propose that buyers will gain less value, buyers view them as losses.
Losses have much greater impact	Because less collaborative sellers are likely to be viewed as less capable and less likable, many buyers will perceive not buying from the collaborative seller as a significant loss in and of itself.

When buyers actively collaborate with sellers in the buying process, it inspires a strong sense of psychological ownership. Buyers who take psychological ownership believe that the priority, approach, case for change—everything—is *theirs*, not *the seller's*.

Psychological ownership grows based on the following three factors:

1. Perception of control, which helps drive buyer commitment to action
2. Depth of knowledge, which drives buyer confidence that "it'll work"

3. Self-investment, which drives perceived value significantly higher, due to what's called the endowment effect, essentially that people value what's theirs more than they value anything that is someone else's

By collaborating, sellers stimulate all three—the buyer's perception of control, depth of knowledge, and self-investment.

Thus, when buyers help shape the priorities for action, they become the buyers' priorities (not the sellers'). When buyers collaborate in the needs discovery, they view the needs as deeply theirs, shaped by them, accurate, and complete. When buyers build the impact case with the seller, they become invested in, and will defend, the impact case to others internally. And, when buyers collaborate to build the solution, they see it as their solution and their preferred path of action.

In sum, by collaborating with buyers, sellers drive actual and perceived value higher, differentiate from other sellers, and win.

Differences in Collaboration— Face-to-Face vs. Virtual Selling

Collaboration is one of the most important factors contributing to the success of top sellers. Consider how collaboration ranks on the Virtual Selling Divergence Scale, a measure of how different a component of selling is when comparing face-to-face vs. virtual selling:

1. Not that much different
2. A little different
3. Somewhat different
4. Different
5. Significantly different

Buyer/seller collaboration is a significant factor in driving relationships and case-making. On the Virtual Selling Divergence Scale, collaboration is **5 out of 5 different.** It's significantly different. Here's how:

Component	Face-to-Face	Virtual Selling
During sales meetings	• Natural, organic ability to collaborate and engage in back-and-forth communication • Collaboration has low physical and psychological barriers (e.g., standing up at a real whiteboard and grabbing a dry-erase marker isn't difficult for most people).	• Both buyers and sellers tend to think of virtual communication as a medium that is more one-way, presentation-oriented than conversation-oriented, resulting in less interaction and collaboration. • Virtual collaboration requires significant mental energy, as there is much more friction in using the technology to interact (e.g., most people would find it much more difficult to use a virtual versus a real whiteboard).
Before/after sales meetings	It is more challenging to engage buyers through technology, as it requires buyers to switch into virtual mode.	Virtual mode is established as the norm, with virtual interactions expected.

Collaboration in a Virtual Selling World

Karl Dunker's most significant contribution to the world of psychology is the concept of functional fixedness. According to Wikipedia,[4] functional fixedness is a cognitive bias that limits a person to use an object only in the way it has been traditionally used. As he puts it, people have a "mental block against using an object in a new way" compared to the way they traditionally perceive the object.

Here's the challenge with virtual collaboration: Both buyers and sellers tend to think of the virtual medium as home for presentations, not collaboration.

When this happens, however, sellers diminish their opportunity to:

- Build rapport and relationships
- Discover and solve to need
- Inspire buyers with new ideas
- Change buyer perceptions about how to approach their challenges
- Drive psychological ownership of the priority and the solution in the buyer
- Meet the engagement threshold needed to keep buyer attention

The option to collaborate online is, however, eminently available to sellers. It's easy now, and getting easier all the time to achieve collaboration virtually. Many sellers will likely catch on soon, but for the time being, it's a huge opportunity to get ahead of the growing trend for those sellers willing to take the lead and collaborate.

Interestingly, there's quite a body of research to suggest that for the sellers who pull it off, online collaboration can be *even more impactful than face-to-face.*

As noted in the *HBR* article "Collaborating Online Is Sometimes Better than Face-to-Face," online collaboration has a number of benefits, including solving time problems, distance problems, and communication problems:[5]

- By solving time problems, online collaboration creates the benefit of 24/7 production cycles
- By solving distance problems, it enables newly diverse teams
- By solving communication problems virtual collaboration allows us to work together in ways that tap into a broader set of skills and capacities

The author also notes that online collaboration can accommodate a broad variety of communication and work styles. For example, some people like to remain quiet in live meetings, but when they are able to mull things over and express themselves through writing rather than by speaking, they not only interact with more vigor, they provide ideas that move the conversation forward.

Before we dive into specifics, consider the following general observations of how the most skilled sellers collaborate:

- **Keep it simple** *for the buyer*: If you're thinking you need to learn or teach sophisticated technology, think again. Collaborating virtually is 90 percent the seller driving the conversation toward collaboration, and 10 percent technology. Most of the technology consists of very simple tools that most buyers and sellers are already using.

- **Keep it natural:** Don't collaborate for collaboration's sake. Think about where collaboration would be most helpful and weave it in. Just as sellers trying too hard to be liked aren't likable, sellers trying too hard to collaborate do just the opposite; they shut buyer interaction down.

- **Request, don't require:** You may suggest that a buyer engage with you at some point, but don't require it. Your goal is to draw a buyer into the seduction of your value, not force them elsewhere if they don't want to fill out your survey, mark up a draft document, or join a virtual brainstorm session with you.

Approaches and Use Cases

Collaboration Approaches	Use Cases
• Virtual Whiteboarding • Surveys and Polling • Document Reviews • Ongoing Conversation	• Prospecting • Needs Discovery • Needs Driving/Inspiring with Ideas • Solution Crafting • Solution Presentation • Negotiation • Proposal Presentation • Account Development • Winning the Sale—Win Labbing

Virtual Whiteboarding

Virtual whiteboarding is simply working on the same document visually with a buyer simultaneously and collaboratively. Like all collaboration, once you suggest or begin a virtual whiteboard session, you re-engage buyers as their attention sharpens like a student in a university classroom who has just been called on by the professor.

A lot of sellers are intimidated by virtual whiteboarding, but they don't have to be. From a technical perspective, here are four ways to do it:

1. Use a native virtual whiteboard such as Miro, Stormboard, MURAL, or Limnu. For the most part, they take only a few minutes to get going, and in an hour of exploring, you'll be quite proficient. If you want to be whiteboarding in seconds, try Whiteboard Fox. It's literally click-and-whiteboard.

2. Use the whiteboard that comes embedded in your virtual meeting software. The feature is included in most popular platforms (e.g., Zoom, Webex, Skype for Business, and Microsoft Teams). If you want to give it a try, call a friend and practice.

3. Annotate. Most online screen-sharing software will allow you and your buyers to annotate a screen. You may show a slide with space for people to write on it, and they can simply write.

4. Screen journal. Most people think whiteboarding needs to be completely interactive, with the other person having real-time access to screen controls. In fact, in most in-person whiteboarding, only the salesperson is at the whiteboard as a facilitator. The best salespeople will invite buyers to the whiteboard to share their thoughts. Sellers can do the same if they are, say, taking notes in a word processor or slide software, since all they need to do is grant screen control to the other person, which enables them to type live on the other person's computer. More than one person can type at the same time.

Here are a variety of ideas for how you can use virtual whiteboarding across the sales cycle.

Needs Discovery

Type: Screen Journal. Put up an image that summarizes the big-picture needs your buyer may have. It could be simple (like our example here) or more detailed. Choose whatever it needs to be to prompt your buyer to talk about their needs.

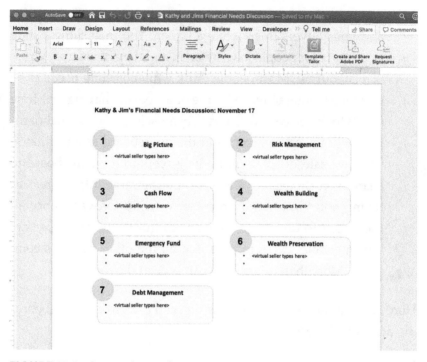

FIGURE 10.1 Screen Journal

In an in-person meeting, it's common for a seller to stand up and write on a real whiteboard, but it would be odd to type notes in a document on a computer, and project it on a screen as the meeting went on.

In a virtual meeting, it's not just natural, it's engaging, impressive, helpful, and time-saving to do so. After the meeting you can simply send the buyer the notes as you took them, and upload everything directly to your CRM, without needing to retype them.

Solution Crafting

A common piece of historical advice in the world of consultative selling was to ask questions to uncover needs, then put together options and ideas for how to tackle them.

Two problems would often crop up:

1. Sellers would uncover the needs—what was wrong and what the buyers wanted—but they wouldn't spend enough time figuring out why the problems were there in the first place. Root cause analysis was weak.

2. When developing options for how to solve the problems and how to ensure success, it's *better to develop the solutions together.*

In RAIN Group training programs, we teach sellers how to lead whiteboarding sessions to fix these problems. Here we share how you can do it through online collaboration. This example assumes you've had an initial needs discovery and shared your summary with the buyer. The next step you suggest is a deeper dive discovery session (with at least one business leader and one technical leader who can weigh in on the issues the desired new reality, and the approaches for going forward).

After welcoming everyone to the session, you could whiteboard as follows: Writing simply with a virtual pen and using the basic features of the software, start with a statement of the problem such as how change is undeniable.

FIGURE 10.2 Whiteboarding the Statement of the Problem

Then share the current state and new reality you gleaned from your initial conversation, and ask, "Does anyone have anything they'd like to add or change?" and "Looking at the suggested metrics on the right, do we have the correct ones and the correct targets?"

FIGURE 10.3 Whiteboarding the Current State and New Reality

The buyer may say something like, "I don't think we could get to less than $11 per user and achieve what we're looking for." If that's a reasonable target, even if it would be a tantalizing opportunity, you might say, "Let's leave that for now and see if we can come up with something that gets us there or close to it."

If they have items to add, take notes. Make changes. Let them write ideas. When you are settled here, move on by drawing a box with the word "Why?"

FIGURE 10.4 Whiteboarding the "Why"

Then ask, "Looking at the current state, let's talk about why we're here. What are your assumptions about what's making all of this not work right? This is important because when we solve the problem, we want the solution to be both effective and durable."

They can either share thoughts as you scribe, or you can ask them to use the whiteboard feature to write problems on sticky notes and put them on the screen until the discussion peters out. As you do, you can consolidate the notes and pare them down to the bare minimum that still represents their reasoning.

As you do this, you might have, on your second screen, your list of thirty-two questions across five categories that can prompt buyers about challenges and issues they might not be coming up with themselves.

Then, move onto solution crafting with a much deeper understanding of what you're actually trying to solve for. Same thing: You can scribe as they talk, they can type on the screen, or they can put up sticky notes. Just like a real whiteboard.

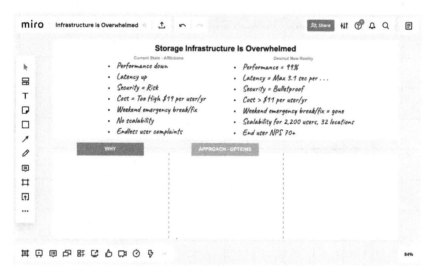

FIGURE 10.5 Whiteboarding Options for the Approach

You could, again, on a separate screen, have a list of the common components of the solution: all the different pieces that come together to make the right mix. This provides the virtual seller two advantages: 1) you can recall all the different components to bring forward for the solution and 2) you can share these different components with the buyer visually to give them ideas of what's possible.

Finally, you can lead a discussion on implementation, making sure that they achieve the goals they want to achieve. You might put up "Implementation: Ensuring Success" and say "55 percent of implementations take seven months longer than expected, and 63 percent don't live up to expectations 18 months later. What do you think needs to happen here to make sure we get this right from the get-go?"

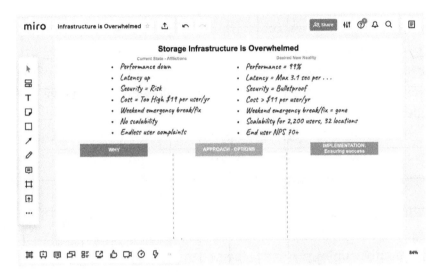

FIGURE 10.6 Whiteboarding the Implementation

As you do this, you're not only building desire to act—because the buyers see their own root cause analysis, having worked on crafting the approach themselves—but are building confidence that "it'll work" when they think through how to tackle implementation.

Take care, by asking these questions, you are not leaving everything in their hands. It's up to you during the discussion to use good selling skills, guiding them down the right path and to the right solution. If they say something that might not be true, dig into that with them. If they say something isn't possible, when in fact it is, or they think something will be really easy and it isn't, address it.

If they're missing key areas, bring them up yourself. The idea is to balance Advocacy and Inquiry as you sell, provide ideas and insights, and guide the discussion to the best outcome.

Co-develop the ROI Case

It's common for sellers to plug some assumptions into a before-and-after calculator and share it with buyers, showing a tremendous ROI.

But when buyers build the ROI themselves—changing the assumptions and calculating the ROI numbers—the ROI message becomes much more powerful. Here's how it might play out: You simply build it with buyers in real time, allowing them to give you ideas for what to change, and see how it comes out.

Visit the *Virtual Selling* book tools section of the RAIN Group website to watch a video example of a collaborative ROI case development (http://raingrp.com/VS-BookTools).

Winning the Opportunity

An advanced technique some sellers use is walking through a complete opportunity plan with their champion to make sure that all components—the needs, the case for change, the buyers involved and their concerns, possible objections, positioning against the competition, action plan, and more—are as tight as possible.

You can either walk them through it live and edit it together, or share it with them via document-share and ask them to go through it and mark it up.

If your opportunity plan is buyer-focused, and your buyer is open to that type of collaboration, it can help place you in the best position to get everything right and win.

Visit the *Virtual Selling* book tools section of the RAIN Group website for a blank copy of the RAIN Group Sales Opportunity Plan you can use generally, as well as in your collaborations with buyers.

Additional Ideas for Virtual Whiteboarding

- Any presentation: Whether it's an idea presentation, a potential solution, or a proposal presentation, you can annotate the screen at any time, and allow others to do the same. They can circle what they like, put up question marks, or make comments. Ask them to challenge you if they have doubts. (Because, if they do, you want to know.) As with all virtual selling, you need to constantly meet the high engagement threshold and involve your buyers. Annotating presentations can help you do this at any time.

- Negotiation: As you walk through ideas—for example, to come up with key terms, figure out new possibilities to achieve your objectives, and overcome objections—you can scribe on a whiteboard, get all the issues out, and agree on points before or after you are done.
- Ideas sessions to grow accounts: Ideas sessions to drive value, what we call Value Labs, are a common live conference room whiteboarding activity. You can use virtual whiteboards to lead the same kind of session.
- What's powerful here, and similar to needs discovery or solution crafting, is you can leave the whiteboard up. No need to write "do not erase" or take pictures of it. What many buyers say, after these sessions is, "We need to invite Jane Smith to see this and weigh in." It's there, you and your customer can walk Jane through, and she can join the whiteboarding process.

While virtual whiteboarding is one of the most engaging ways to collaborate online, there are a variety of other ways to collaborate that can be equally powerful throughout the selling process, including the following.

- **Interactive Document Reactions:** After you write your needs summary, build draft solutions, or build proposals, you can share them via one of the many document-sharing software systems available (e.g., Microsoft Teams and 365 or G Suite) and ask buyers to log in and provide their comments and questions.

The key here is to ask the buyers which document systems they use and *use theirs*. If they work natively in one document-sharing suite, it's unlikely they'll want to work in yours. You can also send documents directly to them (or better yet, build a curated online document center for them) and they can mark it up and send it back with feedback.

- **Curated Online Document Sharing:** All of these—whiteboards, documents, collateral, videos, proposals—anything that's relevant to the buyers, can be housed in a curated online document-sharing system such as DocSend or SmartRooms. Use these tools and you'll know who's downloading, who's visiting, and what people are finding interesting to review versus what they're not paying attention to. There are two advantages to using curated online document-sharing software: 1) you can give buyers a place to go to interact with the documents, and see where they are interacting, and 2) you can get a sense of how engaged the buyers might be overall.

- **Real-time Polling:** Let's say you have five people on a needs discovery call. Build real-time polling into your meeting flow. When it comes time to ask if, say, five areas are important or not, you can say, "I've put up a poll on the screen of five areas that many of our clients find important. Go ahead and click the ones you think are important, and we'll see what everyone thinks."

  If everyone agrees, that's good! You can move forward knowing everyone is on the same page of what to solve for. If the various stakeholders disagree, that's good, too! Then you can lead a discussion and see if you can help everyone get on the same page so you can move forward with clarity.

- **Surveys:** Surveys are a significantly underused collaboration tool in selling. Let's say you sell operational efficiency consulting and technology to businesses. If the company has seventy-seven managers who could weigh in on the untapped areas where you could find efficiencies, build a survey to collect data and comments, then present it to your buyers. This can help you identify the areas everyone thinks will be most fruitful and can build the case for change.

We could easily write a book (and we might) on virtual collaboration. Even though, due to functional fixedness, people think of the virtual world as being more appropriate for one-way communication, it's a fact that ways to collaborate virtually are limited only by a seller's imagination.

Chapter 10 Key Takeaways

- **Collaboration inspires a strong sense of psychological ownership in buyers.** The virtual medium lends itself to **one-way** communication; it takes effort and focus to drive collaboration, but it can be done, and is very powerful when done well. The most skilled sellers collaborate by:
  - Keeping it simple for the buyer
  - Keeping it natural
  - Requesting, not requiring

- **Virtual collaboration ideas are expansive.** Some outlined in this chapter are just a few examples:
  - Shared whiteboarding
  - Opportunity planning
  - ROI case building
  - Surveys
  - Polls

CRUSHING YOUR SALES GOALS: UNLOCKING THE PRODUCTIVITY CODE

Virtual Selling Changes How You Work

Ever hear of Nir Eyal? He's the author of *Hooked: How to Build Habit-Forming Products*.[1] Most people haven't heard of him. You know who has? Everyone at every technology, gaming, and social media company trying to get you addicted to their products that you use when you're sitting at your computer—like you do all day virtual selling.

Two decades ago, selling was very different. Think about prospecting as an example. It was just you, the phone on your desk, and the ticking clock in the background. Every once in a while, you might hear a side conversation or colleagues on the phone. But for the most part, it was quiet—except for that ticking clock.

Nowadays we all have email, texting, Facebook, LinkedIn, Snapchat, Instagram, multiple phones, YouTube, and everything we could ever read including up-to-the-minute news, always available, morning, noon, and night, on our desks and in our pockets. As if simply being aware it's there is not enough, to remind us, we distract ourselves and everyone else at all hours with constant beeping, buzzing, dinging, whirring, and chirping.

Indeed, we are hooked. Deloitte found in a recent study that people collectively check their smartphones upwards of eight billion times per day.[2] Across all age groups, people checked their phones fifty-two times a day in 2018—up from thirty-three times a day in 2014—for two hours and fifty-one minutes (that's 171 minutes a day!).[3]

No question, we live in a world of ever-increasing distraction. As reported in the *New York Times*, people are distracted, on average, every eleven minutes.[4]

The effects on our productivity of this relatively recent change are mind-blowing:

- Researchers discovered that interruptions make you twenty percent dumber.[5]
- Even three-second distractions double workplace errors.[6]
- When people get interrupted, it takes on average twenty-three minutes and fifteen seconds to get back to task.[7]
- After only twenty minutes of interrupted performance, people reported significantly higher stress, frustration, workload, effort, and pressure.[8]

No question; distraction is bad and getting worse. (Thanks, Nir.)

For some sellers, the distraction that comes with virtual selling has ramped up tenfold: Fewer face-to-face meetings in conference rooms; it's all on a computer. Fewer drives to buyer sites, drives to the office, and plane rides; now it's a computer. Coffees, lunches, breakfasts, networking meetings—computer, computer, computer.

Before the recent, dramatic shift to virtual selling, most sellers already had phone, computer, media, and general habits that allowed them to be distracted constantly. A seller's life is rapid task switching, answering the phone when it rings, replying to customer emails, responding to last minute RFPs, back-to-back-to-back meetings, and the like.

These behaviors were killing productivity before virtual selling ramped up like crazy.[9]

Now, these productivity killers are multiplying faster than Tribbles.

Making the shift to virtual selling means selling differently: without planes, without conferences, without lunches and coffees, and without visiting buyers in their offices. It also means *working* without planes, conferences, meals, and visiting buyers at their offices. For many, it also means working from home instead of at an office.

Thus, it's contingent upon virtual sellers to take the lead, and make the choice to become extremely productive in an environment often conducive to the opposite.

For virtual sellers to succeed they must be masters of proactivity, choose the right activities to work on, manage very different schedules and workdays, and focus when it's time to do so. Those sellers that recognize the need to acquire a new set of work habits, and take the lead on managing *themselves* in a different way, enjoy much more success than those that don't.

In this chapter of *Virtual Selling*, we will illustrate a proven system to become extremely productive by introducing you to the habits and hacks of The Productivity Code. The Productivity Code is an easy to adopt time management, focus, and concentration system that has been proven around the globe to drive remarkable increases in personal productivity.

THE STORY OF THE PRODUCTIVITY CODE

I (Mike) found myself in a work location for years that I never expected: in a cardiac ward caring for my son at Boston Children's Hospital. To say that working in a pediatric cardiac intensive care unit was challenging is the understatement of the century.

In 2011, my wife Erica, who also works at RAIN Group, became pregnant with our first son, Ari. Ari was diagnosed in utero with a very serious heart condition. At the same time, we started RAIN Group. We intended to take time off of work after Ari was born until he came home from the hospital, but what we thought would be a few weeks stay turned out to be the better part of the first year of Ari's life.

As a matter of survival (we needed to keep the business going and keep our health insurance active), when Ari was resting and recovering, we had no choice but to work. Living in and out the hospital then continued for the better part of the next six years.

What we learned about how to focus, be productive, and maintain boundaries between our work and "home" life eventually coalesced as The Productivity Code.

The underlying concepts of The Productivity Code eventually became the subject of a large global study on work habits and the productivity of 5,000 people (and growing), which has now helped countless thousands of others learn to become extremely productive even when dealing with enormous challenges, and with a variety of priorities competing for their time.

Research presented throughout this chapter is derived from that study, *The Extreme Productivity Benchmark Report,* which is available in the *Virtual Selling* book tools section of the RAIN Group website (http://raingrp.com/VS-BookTools), and the subject of the book ~~Not~~ *Today: The 9 Habits of Extreme Productivity* (BenBella, 2021).

Differences in Productivity— Face-to-Face vs. Virtual Selling

Selling and potentially working virtually is a significant factor and change in managing yourself. On the Virtual Selling Divergence Scale, productivity is 5 out of 5 different. It's significantly different.

1. Not that much different
2. A little different
3. Somewhat different
4. Different
5. Significantly different

Here's how.

Component	Face-to-Face	Virtual Selling
Motivation	• Hustle and urgency of going from meeting to meeting drives proactivity • Working at an office helps feed off of peer energy • Rhythm of work and habits driven by office culture	• Less travel and commuting creates more unstructured time that can lead to procrastination • Working alone, and without face-to-face contact with managers, can sap motivation • Must create own work rhythm and productive habits; relationship with sales manager on different rhythm with different interaction dynamics (applies to focus and execution as well)
Focus	• Forced focus of in-person meetings (no computers, no phones—just you and the buyers for both of you) • Clear boundaries between work and personal life • Easier to find personal workspace	• Tele-meetings allow for distraction of emails, phones, and other issues; shutting the meeting off is a click away • Boundaries between work and home can blur • Difficult to find spaces to focus and fight distraction

Component	Face-to-Face	Virtual Selling
Execution	• Being out and about, with periodic times on computer; some find meetings tiring, others find them energizing • Travel and commuting kill time that can be used to fuel energy • Team interactions and meetings take away time, but drive schedule and focus	• Out and about much less, much more time with the computer; some find computers and screens tiring, others find them energizing • Saved time travel to and from meetings and commuting means more time to fuel your energy • Fewer team interactions to pull you away from distracted time

SELLING WHEREVER YOU WORK

Sellers who switch from working in an office to working from home have the added challenge of transitioning to selling virtually and working virtually. While this chapter has many references to working from home, we realize only some virtual sellers do that.

Regardless, the tactics and hacks presented in this chapter succeed regardless of your work location.

Driving Productivity in a Virtual World

The Productivity Code and 9 Habits of Extreme Productivity

The Productivity Code is built on the following 3 Keys and associated habits:

1. Manufacture Motivation: Create motivation and proactivity at will, even when you might not be feeling it when you get started
2. Control Your TIME: Focus on the right activities, and become impossible to distract
3. Execute in the Zone: Get the maximum amount done in the least amount of time through achieving the state of flow

We cover each of the 3 Keys and associated habits in the brief chapters that follow.

FIGURE IV.1   The Productivity Code Model

CHAPTER 11

KEY 1.
MANUFACTURE MOTIVATION

To learn more about The Productivity Code visit the *Virtual Selling* book tools on the RAIN Group website for free content or pick up a copy of *Not Today: The 9 Habits of Extreme Productivity* (BenBella, 2021).

Motivation historically has been thought of as something intrinsic—you have it or you don't.

New research shows that we all have motivation inside of us, we just need to draw it out. We can grow it like a skill. Build it like a muscle. The first three habits of The Productivity Code will teach you how.

Habit 1: Recruit Your Drive

How you think about the origin of any task makes a tremendous difference in how motivated you feel to do it.

An analysis of forty-one different studies on the effect of choice on motivation found that "choice enhanced intrinsic motivation, effort, task performance, and perceived competence."[1]

The reasons? Choice makes the task *meaningful* and maximizes *psychological ownership** of getting it done and done well.

If you want to make your virtual selling work, or any task, meaningful to you, you need to first choose your New Reality. In

---

* See the next chapter for a more detailed overview of the concept of psychological ownership.

sales, you want your *buyers* to see what their New Reality can be so their motivation to achieve it is as strong as possible. You also need to do this for yourself. What's your New Reality? What do you want? What are your goals? Where are you trying to get to?

If you're happy with the status quo, you don't need to do anything differently. But if *you want* something else—to be in a different place than you are now—you need to know where you're headed. Then you need to ask yourself, "Why?" Why do you want to be there? Why engage with your New Reality?

If you're connected to the "why" of what you're doing, you can bear almost any "what" to get there.

Once you know your New Reality and your why, write them down. A study of over 450,000 sales people shows that, 82 percent of the top 10 percent in sales performance have written goals. Only 34 percent of the bottom 10 percent of performers do.[2]

After you've written your goals, you can build a specific action plan to achieve them.

A study published in the *HBR*[3] focused on what most motivated salespeople. They researched four factors:

1. Task clarity: whether people knew very specifically what to do with their time
2. Intrinsic factors: whether people came to the job naturally highly motivated
3. Compensation and incentives: how much and how people were paid
4. Management: whether supervisors could fire up their teams

The most motivating factor they found?

Task clarity.

When you know your goals (your New Reality) and connect them to your actions, those actions are meaningful. They feel less like drudgery *even if they are the same actions that drained you in the past.*

When you choose where you want to go, the actions you need to take to get there become your choice. For many virtual sellers, this could mean prospecting, learning how to collaborate with buyers online, or writing a marathon of proposals.

A strong focus on weekly actions—just twenty minutes a week planning them—will focus what you do, give you task clarity, and help you feel motivated to do it.

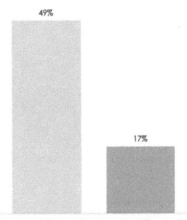

49%

17%

I plan my priorities and work activities weekly so I can be deliberate about my work choices.

The Extremely Productive ■ The Rest

FIGURE 11.1   Plan Weekly Actions

Finally, don't just plan your actions weekly, track them weekly with someone else.

Researchers at Dominican University studied workplace achievement of objectives set in four-week blocks.

One group didn't track their objectives weekly or share their results with a partner. Only 43 percent of them achieved those objectives.

Another group wrote their objectives and tracked weekly with a colleague. Seventy-six percent of them achieved their objectives— almost *double* the success.

We tested this with many sellers in our Extreme Productivity study. In fact, the Extremely Productive (which we refer to as the XP), are 2.9 times more likely to plan actions weekly and track them with a colleague.

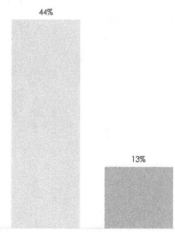

I track progress weekly on how I am doing relative to achieving my short-term objectives.

The XP The Rest

FIGURE 11.2 Track Progress Weekly

Planning actions and tracking them with an accountability partner (your sales coach, a peer—anyone) is a powerful force in recruiting your drive. When you sell virtually, it's even more important because you don't necessarily have a manager or peers on your left and right at the office helping you stay accountable. Take the lead and do it yourself, and you'll be well on your way to recruiting your drive.

Habit 2: Ignite Your Proactivity

Twenty percent of people are chronic procrastinators.[4] These folks even have a name: procs (rhymes with Crocs). Everyone is a periodic procrastinator. When something people want to do or know they need to do seems difficult and requires a lot of energy, they avoid it.

For virtual sellers, procrastination can be that much more common since you often work by yourself, in front of your computer, with a lot of difficult tasks in front of you that require proactivity over the long term.

We've identified three catalysts that can help you get started on important tasks by *lowering the activation energy* perception and actual requirements. Try them and you will ignite your proactivity.

> 20 percent of people are chronic procrastinators. Everyone is a periodic procrastinator.

Put It Here and You'll Do It

A study in the *British Journal of Health Psychology* analyzed the results of people who committed to the following:

> During the next week, I will partake in at least 20 minutes of vigorous exercise on «DAY» at «TIME OF DAY» at/in «PLACE».

Group 1 committed to "keep track" of whether they exercised.

Group 2 committed to "keep track and read a pamphlet on the benefits of exercise."

Group 3 committed to "keep track, read a pamphlet, and make a plan for when and where to exercise."

In Group 1 (the control group), 38 percent of people exercised at least once per week. Group 2 (the motivation group) exercised weekly at a rate of 35 percent. Group 3 (the intention group), exercised weekly at a rate of 91 percent.

These results have been proven time and again in different psychological studies and through our own work with clients. We know this:

If you put it on your calendar, you're much more likely to do it.

Not everything should go on your calendar, just the important things: the areas where you want to invest your time that will reap you outsized returns in the form of achieving your goals.

Calendaring Investment time is very powerful for sellers. Maybe it's prospecting, or an online collaboration session with stakeholders at your top account, or building an amazing virtual proposal presentation to win a big opportunity. If it's important, block off time in your calendar to do it. XP sellers are 2.7 times more likely to calendar their tasks.

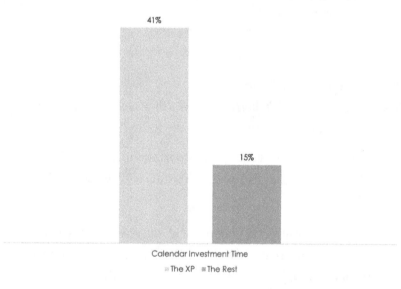

FIGURE 11.3 Calendar Investment Time

Proactivity Catalyst #1: Calendar Investment Time[**]

USE POSITIVE SELF-TALK
Often what holds people back from being proactive is negative self-talk. To change the belief, change how you talk to yourself.

[**] We get more specific about investments and define TIME in the next chapter.

Negative self-talk	Positive self-talk
I'm terrible at leading virtual sales meetings.	I need to learn what a great sales meeting looks like, then I can learn to lead one.
Virtual selling is not as good as selling live.	Virtual selling can be even better if I take the lead and master it.
It's impossible to build strong relationships with people without meeting them in person.	I can find ways to strengthen and deepen my relationships with buyers if I am proactive and creative.
I'm not good at this and won't be.	I'm not good at it yet, but I will learn and get there.
I can't concentrate with all the distractions.	If other people can tune out distractions, so can I; I must research how [or just keep reading].

Henry Ford's old adage still holds true: "Whether you think you can or you think you can't, you're right." Positive self-talk will help you be more productive all around.

Regarding proactivity, positive self-talk goes one step further.

If you think you can't, you *won't even bother to start*. And if you think you can, you're more likely to get to it.

Proactivity Catalyst #2: Talk to Yourself

RAPID ACTIVATION TALK

Positive self-talk can get you in the success mindset. There is, however, a different kind of self-talk that will help you get started on important activities with all the extra time you have virtual selling vs. in-person selling. We call it Rapid Activation Talk.

Here's what happens. You think, "I should brainstorm strategies to drive account growth for the next hour." Then, seconds later, the emotion center of your brain tries to sabotage you. "This is hard. I don't feel ready. I can do it later (but I won't). Something else—like skimming Facebook or checking email—is more important (even though it isn't)."

In order to preempt the feeling part of the brain from shutting you down, you need to head it off at the pass, and you only have a few seconds to do it.

Rapid Activation Talk is the solution. All you have to do—like any school-age kids egging their friends on to race—is say "3... 2... 1... Go!" and immediately get started. There are various ways to practice Rapid Activation Talk. It's worked well for so many people there's an entire book dedicated to it.[5]

For all the various researchers and authors who have their versions of Rapid Activation Talk, the point is universally the same: You have a short amount of time to get started before your brain tells you "that's too hard."

Proactivity Catalyst #3: Say "3... 2... 1... Go!"

Habit 3: Reengineer Your Habits

You have to do things differently, and do different things, if you want different results.

And, if you want to do something—anything—different, you have to understand habits and understand how to change them.

Here we boil it down for you.

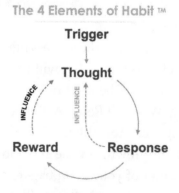

The 4 Elements of Habit ™

Trigger

Thought

INFLUENCE

INFLUENCE

Reward — Response

FIGURE 11.4   The 4 Elements of Habit™

Habits are comprised of the following four elements:

1. **Trigger:** Something happens that cues a sequence of actions you tend to do. For example, your phone buzzes in your pocket.
2. **Thought:** The cue triggers a thought, even if it's fast or sub-conscious. The thought might be, "I should reach into my pocket now to check the message."
3. **Response:** You take an action. Hand goes into pocket, takes phone, you check message.
4. **Reward:** This is your gain or payoff. "Oh great. That report I'm waiting for is in. I'll stop what I'm doing and take a look."

If you want to change this or any habit, you need to change the above.

In one study, researchers noted epilepsy sufferers had trouble remembering to take their medications on time.[6] In fact, before intervention, they only did so 55 percent of the time.

Then researchers asked them to make a "When I, Then I" statement, such as "When it's eight o'clock in the morning and I've finished brushing my teeth, then I will take my prescribed medication."

Those who made the statement increased their compliance taking their meds to 79 percent.

Note that "When I" calls attention to the trigger. The "Then I" statement introduces the thought of what someone should be doing versus something else, making the thought conscious, and directing the response to a different choice.

It's not, however, just "When I, Then I." Add asking yourself, "Will I?"

People who tell themselves to do something (e.g., "When I, Then I") don't do it as often as those who ask themselves if they will.[7]

They both work, so use them together. Define your "When I, Then I" statements so you know what you want to do when. Then, for the most important of your desired actions, ask "Will I?" in the morning. You then give yourself the best chance of doing it.

For example, you might say, "When I turn on my computer in the morning, then I will get right to prospecting and not read news stories." If this is a critical habit for you to change, then ask yourself in the morning, "Will I actually focus on my greatest impact activity and avoid the news stories when I start to work?"

Adding "Will I?" to the "When I, Then I" makes the practice that much more powerful.

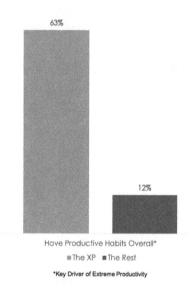

FIGURE 11.5 Overall Productive Habits

Another major factor that influences habits is environment. The environment effects your behavior in two major ways:

1. When you're in a particular place, you tend to do (or not do) specific things.
2. How the environment is designed drives you to do some things and not others.

Perhaps you like to prospect with some energy around you. If so, go to a shared workspace, coffee shop, or an office. But you might like to write sales proposals in a quieter space. Whatever it is, find the location that helps you get your best work done.

The other way to change your environment is to be in the same place, but change conditions.

Let's say you know someone is trying to lose weight.

Do you think it would be a good idea to have a piece of chocolate fudge cake and a box of chocolate chip cookies on their desk?

Open?

Fresh-baked and warm?

With vanilla ice cream ready to be scooped on both?

Probably not. We wouldn't make it fifteen minutes—never mind a day, a week, a month—without giving in.

Many of us want to be less distracted by our phones at work. Phones are the chocolate fudge cake of distractions.

Why then do we leave them on our desks, right in front of us, when we work?

Because we're in sales! That's a convenient excuse to have them next to us, though, as we constantly check messaging and social media.

Try putting your phone in a drawer or across the room *when you need to concentrate*. If it rings you can get up and check it, but you will avoid the constant distraction of looking at it all the time.

35% PRODUCTIVITY INCREASES WITH MULTIPLE SCREENS

Research conducted by Fujitsu Siemens Computers found that workspaces equipped with three screen displays increase productivity by 35.5 percent.

Small changes to your virtual selling environment can make a big difference. Never mind that multiple screens are critical for leading the best virtual sales meetings.[8]

Noise, music, clutter, phones, browsers, inboxes, chairs, computing environment, door open or closed—the list goes on. All these environmental factors affect your productivity one way or another.

The idea behind all of them, however, is the same: Change your environment to change your habits.

Finally, a keystone behavior of extremely productive people is to have a consistent morning routine that starts the day off right. The Extreme Productivity morning ritual goes as follows:

1. Read short-term objectives and actions like your weekly plan.
2. Ask, "How's my mindset?" If it's not good, you won't be productive.[9] Before you get going, use positive self-talk or some of the other hacks shared in this chapter to turn things around.
3. Ask "Will I?" for critical tasks. When you ask yourself *(versus tell yourself) if you will do a critical task* there's a significantly higher percent chance you will.[10]
4. Be better than yesterday. Pick one thing and try to improve.
5. Start with your GIA (Greatest Impact Activity). You'll be surprised by how well a month goes when you do this every day.

Chapter 11 Key Takeaways

- **New research shows** that we all have motivation inside of us, we just need to draw it out. We can grow it like a skill. Build it like a muscle. The first three habits of The Productivity Code will teach you how.

- **Habit 1:** Recruit Your Drive. Motivation is more a skill than an innate have-it-or-don't attribute. You can recruit your drive, building your motivation like a muscle.

- **Choose your New Reality.**
  - Plan actions weekly.
  - Track progress weekly.

- **Habit 2:** Ignite Your Proactivity. How you manage your calendar and your expectations of what you will get done every week drives whether you get it done or procrastinate.
  - Calendar your investment time.
  - Talk to yourself with positive self-talk.
  - Say "3... 2... 1... Go!" to get started on any task.

- **Habit 3:** Reengineer Your Habits.

- **Understand the four elements of habit** (Trigger, Thought, Response, Reward) and you can change habits as you wish.
  - Say "When I, Then I" and add "Will I?" to change your responses and thoughts to triggers.
  - Start your morning right with the Extreme Productivity morning routine.

CHAPTER 12

KEY 2.
CONTROL YOUR TIME

To learn more about The Productivity Code visit the *Virtual Selling* book tools on the RAIN Group website for free content or pick up a copy of ~~Not~~ *Today: The 9 Habits of Extreme Productivity* (BenBella, 2021).

Most time management systems are too complex. They don't need to be. If you do (and don't do) a few simple things and you can reclaim significant lost time, then spend that time the way you want.

If you want to be most productive, you shouldn't just make time management a priority.

You must do the following.

Habit 4: Obsess Over TIME

Where does obsessing over TIME start? With understanding it, tracking how you spend it, and choosing how you should spend it.

4 Levels of TIME

At RAIN Group, we find it instructive to think of time in the following four levels:

1. Treasured
2. Investment
3. Mandatory
4. Empty

Level	Description	Action
Level 4: **Treasured**	Time you hold dear	Take some now, maximize for future
Level 3: **Investment**	Time that generates outsized returns	Increase: prioritize, calendar, maximize
Level 2: **Mandatory**	Time you feel you must spend	Minimize/outsource
Level 1: **Empty**	Time you waste	Eliminate/minimize

FIGURE 12.1 4 Levels of TIME

- **Treasured time** is time you hold dear. This is where we all want to get. For different people it means different things: quality time with loved ones, vacation with friends and family, alone time, sports, and so on. *The key to maximizing happiness and fulfillment is taking Treasured time.*
- **Investment time** is the time you focus on becoming more effective, getting the right things done, and achieving top performance. *The key to success and achieving top performance is maximizing Investment time.*
- **Mandatory time** is time spent doing things you feel you must do (even if, in reality, you don't). *The key to Mandatory time is minimizing or converting it into Treasured or Investment time.*
- **Empty time** is exactly as it sounds: time spent, nothing gained. *The key to Empty time is to eliminate as much of it as you can.*

When it comes to TIME, remember simply to Take T, Increase I, Minimize M, Eliminate E.

Where people tend to spend their time on any given day is a reflection of how they're likely to spend time for months and years to come. Time itself is a collection of habits. If you want to be extremely productive, you first have to understand how you spend your time.

Most people who track their time, even for just two days, find many surprising ways they can make changes.

In fact, the Extremely Productive (The XP) people report having 1.8 more Investment hours available per day than The Rest, and even still, could increase that by another 1.5 hours.

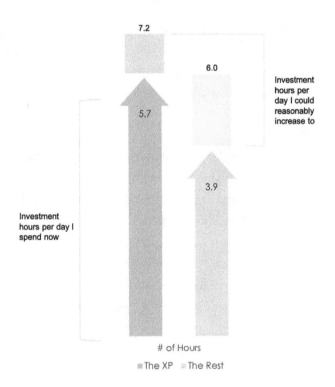

FIGURE 12.2 Investment TIME Analysis

The sooner you figure out where your time is going, the sooner you can start maximizing time spent on what's actually important to you.

The most important of which is your daily Greatest Impact Activity.

> **Greatest Impact Activity (GIA):** The one activity that, should you do it consistently at high quality, will get you the greatest eventual return on your time investment.

Perhaps one of the most commonly noted game-changing hacks in The Productivity Code is not just the concept of identifying your GIA, but putting it first in your day. Do that and 1) you get it done and 2) it tends to lead to more time focusing on Investment activities and less time spent elsewhere.

Habit 5: Say No

- A marketing colleague asks you to join a virtual meeting because they'd value your opinion at the end.
- Your boss messaged for the third time today, this time for a status report update since the one he got two days ago.
- You get a satisfaction survey from the health insurance company about your recent doctor visit.
- A potential client reaches out and wants to talk, but you're pretty sure they won't be a good client even if you win them.

Anything here can kill your time and your ability to take the Investment actions you need to achieve your goals. It's hard to do the thing you know you should.

Say "No."

You might read this list and think, "I'm a good team player. I shouldn't say no to my colleague." "I shouldn't say no to taking a meeting with a potential buyer even if they may not be a good fit."

But are you sure you shouldn't say no?

With your colleague, do you really need to go to the meeting for an hour? Maybe five minutes on the phone will do.

Hour saved.

Be brutal with your priority list. If you have thirty-two priorities, you have none. Get a colleague or coach to help you be brutal and say "No" to the least important, and to feeling responsible for responding to the all noise that comes into your inbox all day.

Our advice here is simple, and powerful: *Do less: If it's not gung ho, it's no.*

PRACTICE SAYING NO

In the opening of this section, we shared ways that people might derail your time. Here are ideas for responding to a couple of them.

BOSS: We know, sometimes you can't just say no. Depends on the boss and the situation. Most people just do the reports or do what's asked. Instead, talk to your boss about how important the report is. You might say, "I'm trying to close the Jones deal. Do you want me to do that or the report?" Have a chat with him to review your priorities. Talk about what the boss needs and see if he can receive it once every other week instead of three times each week. Maybe someone else can do it. The "No" is in there somewhere, tactfully.

POTENTIAL CLIENT: Can't say no? Sure you can. Like with the boss, you can do it tactfully, but do it if it means you won't close the Jones-type deals for fifty times the size because the mosquito deals are eating you and your time alive.

The crucial point about saying no? It's difficult. It's emotional. But it's necessary if you want to focus on your priorities and not attend to other people's.

Habit 6: Play Hard to Get

The world is full of distractions. You must take the lead to actively shut them out. The best way to do that is to play hard to get. When you do, you'll be impossible to distract.

First, turn off all your alerts. With alerts on (ding, buzz, ring), there's no way to avoid constant distraction. Alerts are shackles.

Since virtual sellers are in front of their computers most of the day, the shackles are often that much stronger.

Turn off your alerts, and you'll be free of those shackles. Close and log out of applications that might distract you. Literally put the distractions (like your phone) across the room while you're concentrating. Do this and you give yourself a fighting chance.

Second, signal "Do Not Disturb." Close your door. Put headphones on even if you're not listening to anything. Put up a sign that reads, "On a deadline. Come in if it's an emergency. If not, please check back later."

Third, if you're in a spot in the office where people interrupt you, spend some time working somewhere else if you can. If they can't find you, they won't distract you.

With the exception of turning off your alerts, you don't need to do these all the time but practice these strategies and give yourself the space to focus, concentrate, and get done what you want to get done.

Play hard to get and you'll be impossible to distract.

Chapter 12 Key Takeaways

- **Habit 4 Obsess Over TIME:** Know where your time goes and you will find more, and then devote that to your Greatest Investment Activities (GIAs) that will help you achieve the best return and success. If you want to be most productive, you must understand the 4 Levels of TIME: Treasured, Investment, Mandatory, Empty.
  - Remember to take T, increase I, minimize M, and eliminate E.
  - Start each day with your GIA.

- **Habit 5 Say No:** People and activities will try to derail you from what you should be working on. Significant time loss is preventable if you say "No." Remember, *if it's not gung ho, it's no.*

- **Habit 6 Play Hard to Get:** People and technologies will try to interrupt you. Play hard to get, signal "Do Not Disturb," and turn off your technology alerts so you will be impossible to distract.

CHAPTER 13

KEY 3.
EXECUTE IN THE ZONE

To learn more about The Productivity Code visit the *Virtual Selling* book tools on the RAIN Group website for free content or pick up a copy of ~~Not~~ *Today: The 9 Habits of Extreme Productivity* (BenBella, 2021).

Habit 7: Sprint into the Zone

Typically, with a beam of pride, sellers overwhelmingly tell us in surveys that they are media multitaskers, with five interaction and messaging apps open at once, ready to respond in real time to everyone's needs, pressing or not.

This is good sometimes, when managing multiple communications is in fact the most important activity of the moment, but when sellers need to concentrate, like on prospecting or account growth or proposal development, it's destructive to productivity.

"Media multitaskers pay a mental price, Stanford study shows."[1] The researchers said that multitaskers are "suckers for irrelevancy" and they go on to say why. Not mincing words, are they? The crux: multitasking isn't just bad for productivity—it's very bad.

Not only that, multitasking makes you dumb. It physically shrinks your brain.[2]

So just stop, right? Unfortunately for us multitaskers, multitasking is bad, but it feels good, so it's hard to stop.[3]

Here's how to stop.

If you want to get more done in the time you have, if you want to have that amazing feeling of being extremely productive, then sprint into the zone.

Sprinting is a form of timeboxing. A popular technique in many project management and software development methods, timeboxing allocates a specific time period (or time box), to a pre-planned activity.

> **TIME Sprinting:** Work obsessively on one planned task only for twenty to ninety minutes with a visual stopwatch on, counting up.

The zone (also known as flow) is the mental state where a person performing an activity is fully immersed in a feeling of energized focus, full involvement and enjoyment in the process of the activity. When you're in the zone:

- Time feels suspended—you don't notice it passing and yet it's really flying!
- You feel extreme focus.
- You achieve exceptional clarity of goals, actions, and rewards.
- You're not just happy, you feel euphoric just by focusing on and working on the task.
- The task feels effortless.
- You feel in control and confident that the activity is doable.
- You feel rewarded simply by the fact of engaging the activity.[4]
- If you want to maximize output per work hour, get in the zone.

If you want to get in the zone, establish a daily routine of obsessed planned Sprints. The rules for TIME Sprinting are:

- **Sprint:** Work obsessively on one planned task only for twenty to ninety minutes with a visual stopwatch on, counting up. If you reach ninety minutes, take a break.
- **Relay:** Perform four TIME Sprints in a row with up to six-minute breaks in between. Each four-sprint-in-a-row sequence is a relay.
- **Block distraction; keep a distraction capture list:** If you feel a distraction, don't task switch. Keep a notepad handy and write the distraction down. Return to sprinting on your chosen task.

TIME Sprinting is one of the most powerful and effective strategies of The Productivity Code. If you do it, you need to obsess over it just like you do when deciding what to spend your time doing.

When you are TIME Sprinting, *follow the rules*. Yes, put a timer on. Yes, do absolutely no task switching or media checking. Be impossible to distract when you're sprinting.

When you Sprint you'll get in the zone, achieve flow, and each hour you work will become an amazing hour.

Should you Sprint all the time? No. Lead virtual sales meetings without a timer. Respond to correspondence without a timer. Fifteen minutes between meetings? No timer.

However, if you feel like concentration will help, put the timer on and Sprint.

It makes all the difference.

Habit 8: Fuel Your Energy

Everything we've covered so far about The Productivity Code is useless if you're too tired. If you're sluggish when you're working, your results will be predictably sluggish.

Sure, an energy drink here and there and coffee can give you a boost, but energy, and the stamina to sustain it over long stretches of time, is fuel that drives productivity.

If you want to achieve extreme productivity, fuel your energy.

While time is finite—once it's gone, it's gone—energy is not. It can be renewed and strengthened. While there's a huge body of research and study on maximizing your energy, we summarize it simply as follows.

- **Mind:** Practice positive self-talk and mindfulness to feel energetic and ready to tackle your GIAs.
- **Body:** Eat, sleep, and move to drive energy. Be active.
- **Spirit:** Find your personal path to feel at peace and happy. Find whatever spiritual path that's right for you. Take Treasured time to refuel your psyche.

Here are thirteen scientifically proven ways to boost your energy.

1. Eat protein, decrease carbohydrates. Carbohydrates make you crash.[5]
2. Eat small, frequent meals. Especially at lunch, eating smaller meals is proven to help you boost energy.[6]
3. Be active. Moving increases oxygen flow and releases chemicals in the body that help wake you up and sustain energy. Quick walks (e.g., between TIME Sprints), stretches, and midday workouts drive energy.[7]
4. Get physically fit. Research shows fitness and energy go hand-in-hand. Richard Branson says exercise and being fit doubles his productivity.[8]
5. Drink one cup. Too much coffee or tea can induce crashing, but one cup here and there gives the boost without much of a subsequent dip.[9]
6. Take a nap. Don't power through fatigue. Power nap for 20 minutes or so.[10] Short naps burn away sleep inertia.
7. Get enough sleep. Besides the obvious (feeling tired), not getting enough sleep decreases mental performance. Getting only five hours five nights in a row produces similar effects of having a blood alcohol content of .06.[11]

8. Alcohol and sleep don't mix. If you want a good night's sleep, go light on the alcohol.[12]

9. Try yoga. It might just help you fight depression and anxiety.[13]

10. Practice mindfulness. Meditation is an effective way to fight anxiety and increase energy.[14]

11. Take Treasured time. The mental health benefits of leisure activities include lower levels of depression and improved physical and psychological status.[15]

12. Don't watch excessive TV. It leads lead to snacking and bad health.[16] Bad health reduces energy.

13. Go outside to feel alive. A little bit of air and sky reinvigorates, especially for virtual sellers who used to get outside more.[17]

Habit 9: Right the Ship

Changing habits and being productive isn't easy. We all fall off the wagon. The key is getting back on, and staying on, for longer and longer periods.

If you fall off, here are three strategies to get you back on.

Practice Free Won't

Deeply ingrained habits like constantly checking your phone while working happen almost without thought. The thought is there, but it's so fast that we start doing the behavior without seeming to initiate it consciously.

In the late 1970s and early 80s, Benjamin Libet conducted a series of experiments to see whether conscious thought initiates physical behavior. His experiments showed that some triggers make some behaviors happen seemingly without thought.* He concluded (not without melodrama) that we may not actually have free will.

That's not the interesting part though. What's fascinating is that while conscious thought may or may not cause us to initiate certain

---

* Libet's theories have been challenged by the scientific community, and the controversy continues. However, the point we make is that you can stop a behavior with conscious thought once it's started, however it is initiated.

behaviors, conscious thought can *conclusively cause us to stop that behavior*. So perhaps we have no free "will," but we certainly have free "won't."

In Chapter 11 we outlined how saying "3... 2... 1... Go!" can get you started on an activity. If you want to stop an activity, it works in reverse.

Say "3... 2... 1... Stop!"

Start browsing on Facebook during a TIME Sprint? 3... 2... 1... Stop! Start eating Doritos at 8 p.m. after a good day of healthy eating? 3... 2... 1... Stop! Reaching for your phone while you're concentrating? 3... 2... 1... Stop!

Excessive TV. Drinking too much coffee or alcohol. Rapid media switching. Losing focus. Not starting with your greatest impact activity. Doing something that's better delegated to someone else. Joining an hour-long meeting that, after five minutes, you can't add to or get anything from.

Make Micro Changes

As we discussed previously, getting started on anything takes activation energy. If you know you're getting started on something difficult, it takes that much more energy. We've talked to people who are daunted by the idea of focusing for as long as twenty minutes so they don't start TIME Sprint at all.

Where twenty minutes might seem like a lot, five minutes almost never does. If you're having trouble getting into difficult tasks, make the task smaller. Here you can shrink the Sprint to just five minutes, and lower the activation energy bar significantly.

MICRO CHANGE EXAMPLES

- If something you want to happen isn't happening, make micro changes. For example:

- Having trouble getting into the groove prospecting? Make one call, send one email.

- Having trouble getting started working out? Do three push-ups.

- Want to get good at piano? Take one lesson. Practice once.

- Want to clean the house? Start in one room for five minutes.

- Want to read one business book a month? Get a book and read the first page.

We're not the first to suggest this. The FlyLady has done great work here, too. She's a home-clutter busting expert who gives the following advice: Put a timer on for five minutes and start cleaning a room.[18]

Obviously, you can't finish cleaning your room in five minutes, but few people stop when the timer is up. Once you're in it, you keep going because you're over the activation energy hump, and you're achieving the satisfaction and pleasure from the progress you're making.

Same idea works with TIME Sprints and any seemingly large tasks. Don't go twenty minutes. Go five.

Make micro changes.

Your productivity house will be sparkling clean in no time.

Make a Commitment Contract

Ian Ayres, Jordan Goldberg, and Dean Karlan are Yale economists. They surmised several years ago that people who sign iron-clad commitment contracts would be more likely to stick to a commitment they made to themselves than if they didn't make a contract.

They found that those who make a commitment contract with a referee (i.e., an accountability partner you report to every week) increases chances of success by up to 200 percent. Putting money at stake increases chances of success by up to 300 percent.

They've now studied 400,000 commitment contracts with over $35 million dollars on the line.

According to Goldberg, when a referee is used in the commitment contract, the average success rate is 61 percent for goals related to money and finance.[19] (For those wanting to lose weight, the success rate is a not-too-shabby 47 percent.) When the goal involves using both a referee and a financial stake, the success rate for financial resolutions is 87 percent (and a healthy 73 percent for pound-droppers).

One of the authors of *Virtual Selling* gave it a try the first time to right the ship that was sinking due to an outsized waistline. If he didn't make his weight every week, he had to send money to an organization he despised.

He lost the weight, and now is where he was just after his senior year of high school.

If you want something badly enough—to fill your pipeline, grow your top five accounts, master the advanced virtual meeting technologies to impress buyers—put your money and reputation where your mouth is. Make a commitment contract. Put something at stake. Have an accountability partner.

A commitment contract could give you the incentives (or disincentives) to put you over the top and bring about the change you want.

Chapter 13 Key Takeaways

- **Habit 7 Sprint into the Zone:**
  - **Sprint:** Work obsessively on one planned task only for twenty to ninety minutes with a visual stopwatch on, counting up. If you reach ninety minutes, take a break.
  - **Relay:** Perform four TIME Sprints in a row with up to six-minute breaks in between. Each four-sprint-in-a-row sequence is a relay.
  - **Block distraction; keep a distraction capture list:** If you feel a distraction, don't task switch. Keep a notepad handy and write the distraction down. Return to sprinting on your chosen task.

- **Habit 8 Fuel Your Energy:** You can't be extremely productive if you feel tired and sluggish. Take care of your mind, body, and spirit, and you'll feel energized.

- **Habit 9 Right the Ship:** We all lose focus and fall off the wagon. The secret to long-term extreme productivity is not to be perfect all the time, but to get back at it quickly when you fall into unproductive habits and patterns.
  - Practice free won't; say, "3… 2… 1… Stop!"
  - Make micro changes.
  - Make a commitment contract.

Conclusion

The pursuit of productivity is not new, but for virtual sellers it's more important than ever. In the last several years, distraction has become an epidemic while, at the same time, we all have more demands on our time than ever before and a lot of personal change.

Everyone says it's difficult to change. Everyone is right.

It's difficult to get motivated enough to make the change. It's no easy feat changing how you spend your time. Maximizing output per work hour is so much harder in our increasingly distracted world.

However, if you have the right roadmap, you can manufacture your own motivation, control your TIME, and tune out all distractions while you execute in the zone.

And you'll become extremely productive.

> Visit the *Virtual Selling* book tools on the RAIN Group website (http://raingrp.com/VS-BookTools) to download a one-page summary of The Productivity Code's 3 Keys, 9 Habits, and 27 Hacks for you to print and put up by your desk.

NOTES

Introduction

1. Gavin, Ryan, Liz Harrison, Candace Lun Plotkin, Dennis Spillecke, and Jennifer Stanley. 2020. "The B2B Digital Inflection Point: How Sales Have Changed during COVID-19." McKinsey & Company. McKinsey & Company. April 30, 2020. https://www.mckinsey. com/business-functions/marketing-and-sales/our-insights/ the-b2b-digital-inflection-point-how-sales-have-changed-during-covid-19.

2. Schultz, Mike, Shaby, Dave, and Springer, Andy, *Virtual Selling Skills & Challenges: Buyers Share Where Sellers are Succeeding & Failing*, RAIN Group Center for Sales Research.

Section I

1. Schultz, Mike, Shaby, Dave, and Springer, Andy, *Virtual Selling Skills & Challenges: Buyers Share Where Sellers are Succeeding & Failing*, RAIN Group Center for Sales Research.

Chapter 1

1. Schultz, Mike, Smith, Gord, and Kumar, Vivek, *The Value-Driving Difference: How to Grow Revenue, Improve Win Rates, and Retain Top Sellers through Value*, RAIN Group Center for Sales Research.

Chapter 2

1. Schultz, Mike, and John E. Doerr. 2014. *Insight Selling: Surprising Research on What Sales Winners Do Differently*. Hoboken, New Jersey: Wiley.

2. Woods, Carol. n.d. "Consultative Sales: Definition, Process & Techniques." Study.com. Study.com. Accessed June 10, 2020. http://study.com/academy/ lesson/consultative-sales-definition-process-techniques.html.

3. Cobhan, Phillipson. 2014. "How to Develop a Consultative Sales Approach: 26 Business Sales Experts Share Their Expert Tips." Docurated. Docurated. 2014. http://www.docurated.com/all-things-productivity/develop-consultative-sales-approach-26-business-sales-experts-share-expert-tips.

4. Hoar, Andy. 2015. "Death of a (B2B) Salesman." Forrester. Forrester Research, Inc. April 13, 2015. https://www.forrester.com/report/Death Of A B2B Salesman/-/E-RES122288#.

5. Kim, W. Chan., and Mauborgne Renée. 2005. *Blue Ocean Strategy*. Boston, MA: Harvard Business School Press.

6. "Blue Ocean Strategy." 2020. Wikipedia. Wikimedia Foundation. May 26, 2020. https://en.wikipedia.org/wiki/Blue_Ocean_Strategy.

7. Schultz, Mike, and John E. Doerr. 2014. *Insight Selling: Surprising Research on What Sales Winners Do Differently*. Hoboken, New Jersey: Wiley.

8. Collins, James C., and Jerry I. Porras. 2009. *Built to Last: Successful Habits of Visionary Companies*. New York, NY: Harper Business.

Chapter 3

1. Morantes, E. (2014, January 17). Fuze survey reveals U.S. workforce hampered by multitasking and disengagement. Retrieved June 16, 2020, from https://www.fuze.com/blog/fuze-survey-reveals-u-s-workforce-hampered-by-multi-tasking-and-disengagement

2. Lyons, K., Kim, H., Nevo, S.: Paying Attention in Meetings: Multitasking in Virtual Worlds. In: First Symposium on the Personal Web, Co-located with CASCON, vol. (2005), p. 7 (2010)

3. Frisch, B., & Greene, C. (2020, March 5). What It Takes to Run a Great Virtual Meeting. Retrieved June 16, 2020, from https://hbr.org/2020/03/what-it-takes-to-run-a-great-virtual-meeting

Chapter 4

1. Hotz, Robert Lee. 2012. "Science Reveals Why We Brag So Much." The Wall Street Journal. Dow Jones & Company. May 7, 2012. https://www.wsj.com/articles/SB10001424052702304451104577390392329291890.

2. Krumhuber, Eva, Antony S. R. Manstead, and Arvid Kappas. 2006. "Temporal Aspects of Facial Displays in Person and Expression Perception: The Effects of Smile Dynamics, Head-Tilt, and Gender." *Journal of Nonverbal Behavior* 31 (1): 39–56. https://doi.org/10.1007/s10919-006-0019-x.

Chapter 6

1. Schultz, Mike, Shaby, Dave, and Springer, Andy, *Virtual Selling Skills & Challenges: Buyers Share Where Sellers are Succeeding & Failing*, RAIN Group Center for Sales Research.

2. Schultz, Mike, Shaby, Dave, and Springer, Andy, *Virtual Selling Skills & Challenges: Buyers Share Where Sellers are Succeeding & Failing*, RAIN Group Center for Sales Research.

3. Schultz, Mike, Flaherty, Mary, and Murray, Jason, *Top Performance in Sales Negotiation: Surprising Research on Tactics Sellers and Buyers Use, What Works, and What Doesn't*, RAIN Group Center for Sales Research.
4. Labarre, Polly. 2012. "Marcus Buckingham Thinks Your Boss Has an Attitude Problem." Fast Company. Fast Company & Inc. July 30, 2012. https://www.fastcompany.com/43419/marcus-buckingham-thinks-your-boss-has-attitude-problem.
5. Schultz, Mike, and Doerr, John E., *Rainmaking Conversations: Influence, Persuade, and Sell in Any Situation,* John Wiley & Sons, 2011.

Chapter 8
1. Lee, Aaron. 2016. "30 Legendary Startup Pitch Decks and What You Can Learn From Them." Piktochart Blog. Piktochart. June 21, 2016. https://piktochart.com/blog/startup-pitch-decks-what-you-can-learn/#Canvas.
2. Doshi, Suhail. 2014. "Mixpanel - Our Pitch Deck That We Used to Raise $65M." SlideShare. LinkedIn. December 18, 2014. https://www.slideshare.net/metrics1/mixpanel-our-pitch-deck-that-we-used-to-raise-65m.

Chapter 9
1. Tversky, Amos, Kahneman, Daniel, Judgment under Uncertainty: Heuristics and Biases, *Science*, 27 Sep 1974: Vol. 185, Issue 4157.

Chapter 10
1. Schultz, Mike, and John E. Doerr. 2014. *Insight Selling: How to Connect, Convince, and Collaborate to Close the Deal.* Hoboken, NJ: John Wiley & Sons Inc.
2. Schultz, Mike, Flaherty, Mary, and Murray, Jason, *Top Performance in Sales Negotiation: Surprising Research on Tactics Sellers and Buyers Use, What Works, and What Doesn't*, RAIN Group Center for Sales Research.
3. Schultz, Mike, Flaherty, Mary, and Cluytens, Ago, and Jones, Mike, *Top Performance in Strategic Account Management,* RAIN Group Center for Sales Research.
4. "Functional Fixedness." 2019. Wikipedia. Wikimedia Foundation. December 22, 2019. https://en.wikipedia.org/wiki/Functional_fixedness.
5. Samuel, Alexandra. 2015. "Collaborating Online Is Sometimes Better than Face-to-Face." Harvard Business Review. Harvard Business Publishing. April 1, 2015. https://hbr.org/2015/04/collaborating-online-is-sometimes-better-than-face-to-face.

Section IV
1. Eyal, Nir, and Ryan Hoover. 2019. *Hooked: How to Build Habit-Forming Products.* S.l.: Portfolio/Penguin.

2. Deloitte. 2018. "2018 Global Mobile Consumer Survey: US Edition," PDF.

3. Deloitte. 2018. "2018 Global Mobile Consumer Survey: US Edition," PDF.

4. Sullivan, Bob, and Hugh Thompson. 2013. "Brain, Interrupted." The New York Times. The New York Times. May 3, 2013. https://www.nytimes.com/2013/05/05/opinion/sunday/a-focus-on-distraction.html.

5. Sullivan, Bob, and Hugh Thompson. 2013. "Brain, Interrupted." The New York Times. The New York Times. May 3, 2013. https://www.nytimes.com/2013/05/05/opinion/sunday/a-focus-on-distraction.html.

6. Johnson, Bailey. 2013. " Study: 3-Second Distractions Double Workplace Errors." CBS News. CBS Interactive Inc. January 15, 2013. https://www.cbsnews.com/news/study-3-second-distractions-double-workplace-errors/.

7. Mark, Gloria, Daniela Gudith, and Ulrich Klocke. 2008. "The Cost of Interrupted Work." *Proceeding of the Twenty-Sixth Annual CHI Conference on Human Factors in Computing Systems - CHI '08*, January. https://doi.org/10.1145/1357054.1357072.

8. Mark, Gloria, Daniela Gudith, and Ulrich Klocke. 2008. "The Cost of Interrupted Work." *Proceeding of the Twenty-Sixth Annual CHI Conference on Human Factors in Computing Systems - CHI '08*, January. https://doi.org/10.1145/1357054.1357072.

9. Ghose, Tia. 2013. "Heavy Multitaskers Are the Worst At Multitasking." LiveScience. Future US Inc. January 23, 2013. https://www.livescience.com/26528-multitasking-bad-productivity.html.

Chapter 11

1. Patall, Erika A., Harris Cooper, and Jorgianne Civey Robinson. 2008. "The Effects of Choice on Intrinsic Motivation and Related Outcomes: A Meta-Analysis of Research Findings." *Psychological Bulletin* 134 (2): 270–300. https://doi.org/10.1037/0033-2909.134.2.270.

2. Kurlan, Dave. 2009. "Ultimate Comparison of Top Salespeople versus Salespeople That Fail." Dave Kurlan's Blog - The Authority on Sales Force Excellence. December 7, 2009. http://www.omghub.com/salesdevelopmentblog/tabid/5809/bid/11304/Ultimate-Comparison-of-top-salespeople-versus-salespeople-that-fail.aspx.

3. Doyle, Stephen X., and Benson P. Shapiro. 2014. "What Counts Most in Motivating Your Sales Force?" Harvard Business Review. Harvard Business Publishing. August 1, 2014. https://hbr.org/1980/07/what-counts-most-in-motivating-your-sales-force.

4. Murphy, Heather. 2017. "What We Finally Got Around to Learning at the Procrastination Research Conference." The New York Times. The New York Times. July 21, 2017. https://www.nytimes.com/2017/07/21/science/procrastination-research-conference.html.

5. Robbins, Mel. 2017. *The 5 Second Rule Transform Your Life, Work, and Confidence with Everyday Courage*. Brentwood: Savio Republic.

6. Barker, Eric. 2016. "4 Easy Tricks That Will Make You Productive: Proven Secrets From Robert Cialdini." Barking Up The Wrong Tree. Eric Barker. December 4, 2016. https://www.bakadesuyo.com/2016/12/productive/.

7. University of Illinois at Urbana-Champaign. 2010. "Will We Succeed? The Science of Self-Motivation." ScienceDaily.com. ScienceDaily. June 1, 2010. https://www.sciencedaily.com/releases/2010/05/100528092021.htm.

8. Savvas, Antony. 2009. "Multiple Monitors Boost Productivity by 35.5%." ComputerWeekly.com. TechTarget. February 18, 2009. https://www.computerweekly.com/news/2240088457/Multiple-monitors-boost-productivity-by-355.

9. Amabile, Teresa. 2011. Vimeo. 2011. https://vimeo.com/27022929.

10. Barker, Eric. 2016. "4 Easy Tricks That Will Make You Productive: Proven Secrets From Robert Cialdini." Barking Up The Wrong Tree (blog), December 4, 2016. https://www.bakadesuyo.com/2016/12/productive/.

Chapter 13

1. Stanford University. 2016. "Media Multitaskers Pay Mental Price, Stanford Study Shows." Stanford News. Stanford University. April 16, 2016. https://news.stanford.edu/2009/08/24/multitask-research-study-082409/.

2. Stillman, Jessica. 2014. "Multitasking Physically Shrinks Your Brain." Inc.com. Inc. October 2, 2014. https://www.inc.com/jessica-stillman/study-multitask-ing-physically-shrinks-your-brain.html.

3. Ohio State University. 2012. "Multitasking Hurts Performance but Makes You Feel Better." ScienceDaily.com. ScienceDaily. April 30, 2012. https://www.sciencedaily.com/releases/2012/04/120430124618.htm.

4. Csikszentmihalyi, Mihaly. 2008. *Flow: the Psychology of Optimal Experience*. New York: Harper Perennial Modern Classics.

5. Davila, David G, ed. 2009. "Food & Sleep." SleepFoundation.org. SleepFoundation.org. December 2009. https://sleepfoundation.org/sleep-topics/food-and-sleep.

6. "Eating to Boost Energy." n.d. Harvard Health. Harvard University. Accessed June 9, 2020. https://www.health.harvard.edu/healthbeat/eating-to-boost-energy.

7. Schwarz, Ulrica Von Thiele, and Henna Hasson. 2011. "Employee Self-Rated Productivity and Objective Organizational Production Levels." *Journal of Occupational and Environmental Medicine* 53 (8): 838–44. https://doi.org/10.1097/jom.0b013e31822589c2.

8. Ward, Marguerite. 2016. "Richard Branson Says This Daily Habit Doubles His Productivity." CNBC. CNBC LLC. November 10, 2016. https://www.cnbc.

com/2016/11/10/richard-branson-says-this-daily-habit-doubles-his-productivity.html.

9. Mets, M A J, D Baas, I van Boven, B Olivier, and J C Verster. 2012. "Effects of Coffee on Driving Performance during Prolonged Simulated Highway Driving." Pubmed.gov. U.S. National Library of Medicine. July 2012. https://www.ncbi.nlm.nih.gov/pubmed/22315048.

10. Milner, Catherine E., and Kimberly A. Cote. 2009. "Benefits of Napping in Healthy Adults: Impact of Nap Length, Time of Day, Age, and Experience with Napping." *Journal of Sleep Research* 18 (2): 272–81. https://doi.org/10.1111/j.1365-2869.2008.00718.x.

11. Barnes, Christopher M., and Christopher L. Drake. 2015. "Prioritizing Sleep Health." *Perspectives on Psychological Science* 10 (6): 733–37. https://doi.org/10.1177/1745691615598509.

12. Mann, Denise. 2013. "Alcohol and a Good Night's Sleep Don't Mix." WebMD.com. WebMD LLC. January 22, 2013. https://www.webmd.com/sleep-disorders/news/20130118/alcohol-sleep#1.

13. Boston University. 2007. "Yoga May Elevate Brain GABA Levels, Suggesting Possible Treatment For Depression." ScienceDaily.com. ScienceDaily. May 22, 2007. https://www.sciencedaily.com/releases/2007/05/070521145516.htm.

14. https://www.sciencedaily.com/releases/2007/05/070521145516.htm.

15. Marshall, Joelle Jane. n.d. "How Mindfulness Can Help Boost Your Energy Levels." Dummies.com. Wiley. Accessed June 9, 2020. http://www.dummies.com/health/mental-health/anxiety/how-mindfulness-can-help-boost-your-energy-levels/.

16. Patel, R. Ryan. 2019. "Mental Health Benefits of Leisure Activities." OSU.edu. Ohio State University. February 19, 2019. https://u.osu.edu/emotionalfitness/2017/09/22/mental-health-benefits-of-leisure-activities/.

17. "Fernandez, Emily. 2017. "Excessive TV Watching Leads to Snacking, Bad Health Later in Life, Study Finds." ABC News. ABC. June 22, 2017. http://www.abc.net.au/news/2017-06-22/binge-tv-bad-for-your-health-uq-study-finds/8642888.

18. University of Rochester. 2010. "Spending Time in Nature Makes People Feel More Alive, Study Shows." ScienceDaily. ScienceDaily. June 4, 2010. https://www.sciencedaily.com/releases/2010/06/100603172219.htm.

19. "Back to Basics Mission #09 Five Minute Room Rescue." n.d. FlyLady.net. FlyLady and Company, Inc. Accessed June 9, 2020. http://www.flylady.net/d/back-to-basics/back-to-basics-mission-09/.

20. Woolley, Suzanne. "Fattening Up Your 401(k) Will Be Easier Than Losing Weight in 2018." Bloomberg.com. Bloomberg, January 5, 2018. https://www.bloomberg.com/news/articles/2018-01-05/fattening-up-your-401-k-will-be-easier-than-losing-weight-in-2018?cmpId=flipboard.

A SMALL FAVOR

Thank you for reading our book. Would you mind leaving a brief review on Amazon, Goodreads, or wherever you bought it? It doesn't have to be long—the purpose is to share your opinion. This helps other readers decide if our book might be valuable to them.

Amazon: raingrp.com/VS-Review
Goodreads: raingrp.com/VS-Goodreads

We would really appreciate it.
Mike, Dave, and Andy

Virtual Selling Tools, Tips, and More Bonuses

Throughout this book, we shared a handful of resources to help guide you on your path to virtual selling success. These are the same resources used by our Fortune 500 clients who are thriving in this new sales environment. While you may have finished the book, the value does not stop here. If you have downloaded at least one of the tools at raingrp.com/VS-BookTools, you have already gained access to even more virtual selling tips, resources, and special launch offers. Keep an eye on your inbox for more tools and savings.

Bring an Author to Speak at Your Event

The authors of this book have delivered engaging and thought-provoking keynote speeches to clients at sales kickoffs and industry leading conferences around the world every year.

When we give speeches, we work with our clients to understand the direction the organization is heading and align key messages.

Our keynote speeches are filled with engaging stories, humor, and a clear message. You can expect a presentation that captures attention, is filled with the latest statistics to back up key points, and inspires your sales force to reach top performance.

To book one of the authors for your next event, visit raingroup.com.

ACKNOWLEDGEMENTS

Mike, Dave, and Andy would like to collectively thank the incredible RAIN Group team that contributed to developing and producing this book. Special thanks to Mary, who was masterful with her edits and ideas, and to Aly, Stephanie, Erica, Beth, John, and many others who offered time, energy, skill, and wisdom along the way. Additional thanks to David W., our editors, and others who helped us stay on course, and get the process right. To our many clients, we hope our work helps you and those you support to reach your collective goals, and we thank you for your partnership and loyalty over the years. Last, thank you to our incredible families, who are always so supportive. You are the reason we show up strong every day!

ABOUT THE AUTHORS

Mike Schultz

Mike Schultz is a world-renowned speaker, researcher, and sales expert. He is author of several books, including WSJ Best-seller *Rainmaking Conversations* (Wiley, 2011), *Professional Services Marketing* (Wiley, 2013), *Insight Selling* (Wiley, 2014), *Virtual Selling: How to Build Relationships, Differentiate, and Win Sales Remotely* (2020), and ~~Not~~ *Today: The 9 Habits of Extreme Productivity* (2021).

As President of RAIN Group, Mike has grown the firm into a global leader, named a Top 20 Sales Training Company by Selling Power and Training Industry. In 2020, superior client results earned RAIN Group a Brandon Hall Award for Best Unique or Innovative Sales Training Program and four Gold Stevie Awards for Sales Training Practice of the Year, Sales Training Program of the Year, Sales Training Professional of the Year, and Business Development Achievement of the Year.

Mike and the team at RAIN Group have worked with national and international organizations such as Toyota, Citibank, Canon, Bright Horizons, BDO, Hitachi, Lee Hecht Harrison, Hologic, Optus, and hundreds of others to unleash sales performance.

As Director of the RAIN Group Center for Sales Research, Mike and an analyst team study buying and selling relentlessly. Studies include Virtual Buying and Selling Challenges, Top Performance in Sales Negotiation, Extreme Productivity Benchmark Report, Top Performance in Sales Prospecting, The Value-Driving Sales Organization, What Sales Winners Do Differently, Top Performance in Strategic Account Management, Top Sales Leadership Challenges and Priorities, and The Top-Performing Sales Organization.

Business Week, Forbes, Inc., Entrepreneur, MSNBC, and hundreds of others have interviewed and featured Mike's articles, research, and white papers. He frequently appears on top-ranked radio, TV, and podcast programs to discuss various sales topics and new research findings.

Named an influential sales professional by LinkedIn, Mike has presented at major events, including HubSpot INBOUND, Strategic Account Management Association's Annual Conferences, Sales Leadership Conference, and Sales Operations Institute. In 2019, he was honored as a leading keynote speaker by Top Sales World.

Passionate about raising awareness of congenital heart defects (CHD) and organ donation, blogging at echoofhope.org, the American Heart Association (AHA) of Central Massachusetts honored Mike with the Heart of Gold Award in 2018.

Mike is a graduate of Brandeis University in Waltham, MA with a B.A. in American Studies, and holds an MBA from the F.W. Olin Graduate School of Business at Babson College. He was an adjunct professor at both schools, teaching courses in marketing and sales.

Follow Mike on Twitter @Mike_Schultz and LinkedIn at linkedin.com/in/mikeschultz50.

Dave Shaby

Dave Shaby is an experienced sales, marketing, and business operations expert, as well as author of *Virtual Selling: How to Build Relationships, Differentiate, and Win Sales Remotely* (2020).

With 25+ years of experience leading people and functions focused on improving brand, revenue, profitability, and customer experience, Dave held multiple leadership positions at Bright Horizons (NYSE: BFAM), including SVP of Emerging Growth, SVP of Corporate Marketing, SVP of Business Operations, SVP of Consumer Marketing, VP of Consumer Services, and VP of Operations.

As Chief Operating Officer of RAIN Group, Dave drives company growth and client success for the firm that's been named to Selling Power and Training Industry's Top 20 Sales Training Companies list for numerous years running.

Dave has presented at the Strategic Account Management Association's annual conference and regularly contributes to RAIN Group's award-winning sales blog. His white papers, *5 Most Effective Negotiation Tactics Buyers Use on Sellers* and *The Guide to Sales Training Success*, have been downloaded by thousands of sellers and sales leaders around the globe.

Dave is an acclaimed adjunct faculty member at both Babson College and Brandeis University, where he develops and delivers digital marketing courses for MBA students at the International Business School.

Serving on several boards, including the Westwood Education Foundation, Boston Children's Museum, and Bright Horizons' Foundation for Children, Dave works with and mentors several emerging companies to enhance their growth. In his spare time, he enjoys spending time with his family, watching sports, and traveling.

Dave received his B.A. in Business Administration from Ithaca College in Ithaca, NY and holds an M.A. in Journalism from Northeastern University in Boston.

Follow Dave on LinkedIn at linkedin.com/in/davidshaby.

Andy Springer

Andy Springer is an expert in sales high-performance and author of *Virtual Selling: How to Build Relationships, Differentiate, and Win Sales Remotely* (2020).

As Chief Client Officer of RAIN Group, Andy drives the design and delivery of client results for the firm that's been named to Selling Power and Training Industry's Top 20 Sales Training Companies list for numerous years running.

Andy has worked with hundreds of sales teams to drive long-lasting sales improvement for SME, mid-market, enterprise, and government clients.

Leading many of RAIN Group's highly popular digital seminars on virtual selling topics, Andy is a regular contributor to the firm's award-winning sales blog. His white papers, *9 Principles of Virtual Learning Success* and *The Guide to Sales Training Success*, have been downloaded by thousands of sellers and sales leaders around the globe.

In addition, Andy co-founded two successful consultancies and has been a lead advisor to many thriving start-ups in the Australian business community.

Andy received his B.A. in Business from the University of Newcastle, Australia.

Follow Andy on Twitter @AndyJLive and LinkedIn at linkedin.com/in/andyspringer.

About RAIN Group

RAIN Group is an award-winning sales training and performance improvement company that helps leading organizations improve sales results through in-person and virtual sales training, coaching, and reinforcement. We've helped hundreds of thousands of salespeople, managers, and professionals in more than 75 countries increase their sales significantly.

We can help sales organizations:

- **Implement Sales Training that Delivers Real Results:** RAIN Group's sales training system inspires real change and delivers real results that last. Our rigorous approach includes sales team evaluation, customized training programs, robust reinforcement, and coaching to help you and your team develop sales skills and maximize your results.
- **Grow Your Key Accounts:** At most companies, there's a huge, untapped opportunity to add more value—and thus

sell more—to existing accounts. We help our clients capitalize on these revenue growth opportunities. Whether it's simply increasing cross-selling and up-selling or implementing a major strategic account management program, we can help.

- **Deliver High Impact Virtual Instructor-Led Training:** Training a remote and dispersed sales team is a challenge for many sales leaders. We use a mixture of virtual instructor-led training, interactive digital reinforcement, eLearning, and virtual coaching to deliver award-winning training and results.
- **Implement World-Class Sales Coaching:** We coach sellers, professionals, and leaders individually and in groups to achieve the greatest and fastest increase in sales results. And we train and certify leaders and managers in our RAIN Sales Coaching system. Often, it's RAIN Sales Coaching that truly unlocks the team's potential, and keeps them motivated to produce the best results consistently.

Headquartered in Boston, the company has offices across the U.S. and internationally in Bogotá, Geneva, Johannesburg, London, Mumbai, Seoul, Sydney, and Toronto.

To learn more about RAIN Group, visit raingroup.com.

CPSIA information can be obtained
at www.ICGtesting.com
Printed in the USA
FSHW011619040920
73572FS